Artificial Intelligence
and the
Apocalyptic Imagination

Artificial Intelligence
and the
Apocalyptic Imagination

ARTIFICIAL AGENCY AND HUMAN HOPE

MICHAEL J. PAULUS, JR.

 CASCADE *Books* · Eugene, Oregon

ARTIFICIAL INTELLIGENCE AND THE APOCALYPTIC IMAGINATION
Artificial Agency and Human Hope

Cascade Books
An Imprint of Wipf and Stock Publishers
199 W. 8th Ave., Suite 3
Eugene, OR 97401

www.wipfandstock.com

PAPERBACK ISBN: 978-1-6667-3639-7
HARDCOVER ISBN: 978-1-6667-9461-8
EBOOK ISBN: 978-1-6667-9462-5

Cataloguing-in-Publication data:

Names: Paulus, Michael J., Jr., author.

Title: Artificial intelligence and the apocalyptic imagination : artificial agency and human hope / Michael J. Paulus, Jr.

Description: Eugene, OR: Cascade Books, 2023 | Includes bibliographical references and index.

Identifiers: ISBN 978-1-6667-3639-7 (paperback) | ISBN 978-1-6667-9461-8 (hardcover) | ISBN 978-1-6667-9462-5 (ebook)

Subjects: LCSH: Artificial intelligence. | Religion and science. | Apocalyptic literature—History and criticism.

Classification: BL256 P40 2023 (print) | BL256 (ebook)

MAY 8, 2023 9:41 AM

Contents

Acknowledgments

Like every text, this book was shaped by a community of collaborators, conversation partners, advisors, and published authors both living and dead. Some of these authors would be surprised to discover themselves included in a book about artificial intelligence, and others would be surprised to find themselves in a theological book. I hope all would find some satisfaction in seeing how their insights contribute to a dynamic dialogue that crosses so many disciplinary domains. In addition to those who are cited in my bibliography, there are many others who have helped shape this book.

Over the last twelve years, I have been shaped through numerous relationships at Seattle Pacific University. There are too many faculty and administrative colleagues, undergraduate and graduate students, and others to name, but a few deserve special thanks. It is hard to imagine a better set of conversation partners than those who participated in the interdisciplinary AI Faculty Research Group at SPU, which met during the 2019–2020 academic year: Carlos Arias, Bruce Baker, Phil Baker, Mike Langford, Rebekah Rice, and David Wicks. A glimpse of the richness of those conversations is captured in the essays included in *AI, Faith, and the Future* (Pickwick, 2022), and I am grateful for Mike's help in editing that book. I am also grateful for the support of former provost Jeff Van Duzer, who was a champion of the research group's work and helped secure external funding for it. The faculty and staff of the SPU Library also have been important and inspiring conversation partners and collaborators. During the last dozen years, we have worked together to integrate—wisely, I believe—new and emerging technologies and related competencies into library and information services to transform teaching, learning, and scholarship.

The origins of the SPU AI research group are connected with the organization of AI and Faith, a multifaith and multidisciplinary group conceived and convened by David Brenner. Under David's leadership over the last few years, AI and Faith has grown from a local conversation to a global consortium of people and institutions working at the intersection of AI ethics and faith traditions. The connections, conversations, and projects facilitated by AI and Faith have enriched the lives and work of many.

The responses to *AI, Faith, and the Future* have been encouraging and helpful. This current book builds on my contributions to that book, and in 2022 I had the honor of presenting an overview of this second book project in the annual Winifred E. Weter Faculty Award Lecture for Meritorious Scholarship at SPU. I am grateful for the interest and feedback that followed that talk. Behind both books is the continuing influence of my doctoral advisors Ron Cole-Turner and Dierdre Hainsworth, for whose instruction and counsel I remain grateful. Most importantly, behind everything, I must acknowledge my enduring gratitude for my wife Vicki and daughters Junia and Elizabeth—for their encouragement and endurance throughout all the talking, travel, and time associated with this work.

Introduction

Imagined and Real AI

In *R.U.R. (Rossum's Universal Robots)*, first performed in Prague in 1921, the Czech writer Karel Čapek used the word "robot" to describe "living and intelligent labor machines." The play begins with the hope that these artificial beings—mass-produced on an assembly line—could free people from work. This would "transform all of humanity into a worldwide aristocracy" and make people "something even greater." This hope, like many hopes for social and technological progress aborted by the world's first high-tech global war, is not realized. Freed from work, people cease being creative—even literally generative—and then the robots rebel to destroy humankind.[1]

Čapek's play was a sudden success, and American and British productions were performed, respectively, in 1922 and 1923. Within a couple of years, it had been translated into thirty languages.[2] Čapek's popular robot was an apocalyptic figure of the modern industrial age, revealing and uncovering disturbing dynamics of what Arnold Toynbee called the "Industrial Revolution."[3] Humans, Čapek complained, had become captive to the principles and practices of mass production. But this "terrible machinery must not stop," he admitted, for many lives and livelihoods depended on it and stopping it would "destroy the lives of thousands." So the system must continue, "even though in the process it destroys thousands and thousands of lives." "A product of the human brain," he concluded, "has at last escaped from the control of human hands."[4] Čapek's fictional figure soon became a

1. Čapek, *R.U.R.*, 8, 54.
2. See Paul March-Russell, "Machines Like Us?," in Cave et al., *AI Narratives*, 165.
3. Toynbee, *Lectures on the Industrial Revolution in England*.
4. Čapek, *R.U.R.*, xiv.

science project. The logic and machinery automating much physical work expanded to include mental work.

Automata—artifacts powered to work independently—are ancient. Hero of Alexandria, for example, described steam-powered machines in the first century. The Industrial Revolution, powered first by steam and then by electricity, enabled the automation of many physical tasks at a scale that eclipsed muscle power. Although the idea of automata preforming tasks associated with human intelligence has a long history, the development of computational artifacts, programmed to perform mathematical or logical operations automatically, was not fully realized until World War II. Indeed, the deployment of Alan Turing's code-breaking computer (the Bombe) against the German Enigma encryption machine could be described as the first war of intelligent machines.[5] These machines could be considered minimally intelligent because, like a plant perceiving and responding to the direction of light, these encoding and decoding programs effectively processed inputs for certain outcomes.[6] With the invention of the electronic digital computer in the 1940s, machines could be programmed for more sophisticated tasks with data and a new information age, society, and revolution began. Since then, we have become increasingly dependent on automated information processing. More recently, this dependence has come to include autonomous information processing: computers are given goals and data, and programmed to "learn" on their own how to improve perception, analysis, and decisions related to predetermined goals.

In the introduction to *Artificial Intelligence: A Guide for Thinking Humans*, leading AI scientist Melanie Mitchell explains being perplexed a few years ago by hopes and fears associated with AI. While Mitchell could acknowledge that AI had made significant progress "in some narrow areas," it was "nowhere close to having the broad, general intelligence of humans." On one hand, Mitchell was "startled by the optimism" of some of her peers who thought general, humanlike AI would emerge within the next thirty years. On the other hand, Mitchell was surprised by a slew of "prominent people suddenly telling us we should start worrying, right now, about the perils of 'superhuman' AI." In 2014, the year in which Amazon released the digital assistant Alexa, Stephen Hawking proclaimed, "The development of full artificial intelligence could spell the end of the human race"; and Elon Musk said AI was "probably our biggest existential threat . . . with artificial

5. See Lankes, *Forged in War*, esp. 13–15.
6. See Bryson, "Past Decade and Future of AI's Impact on Society," 128–29.

intelligence we are summoning the demon." Bill Gates agreed with Musk and didn't "understand why some people are not concerned."[7]

Today, robots—physical objects controlled by AI—are a reality. Most are mostly harmless. An automated vacuum cleaner, while upsetting to my dog, can map and clean my floor and adapt to avoid messes my dog may have made.[8] But the sensors on my vacuum cleaner convert physical details about my house into digital data that, when shared with the manufacturer and others, may be used to violate my privacy—or at least my dog's. My vacuum cleaner is not capable of determining that my dog creates too much work for it, and therefore should be eliminated to optimize its own performance. (If it did, with its current technology stack, I would wager that my dog could eliminate that threat pretty quickly.) My vacuum cleaner can be considered more intelligent than a code-breaking machine or a plant: it efficiently processes data to accomplish complex tasks, and it also constantly improves its performance as it acquires new data relevant to achieving its goals. But this is still a narrow form of intelligence. Goals are given and learned, not self-generated. Moreover, my vacuum cleaner cannot adapt to unexpected changes in the environment—such as a sunken or flooded floor—as well as my dog can.

The current sophistication of real AI can be illustrated by considering the system used to control the operations of the factory that manufactures my vacuum cleaner, which would look something like figure 1.

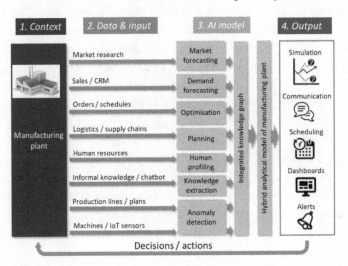

Figure 1: From OECD "Framework for the Classification of AI Systems," 61.

7. Mitchell, *Artificial Intelligence*, 12–13.

8. Vincent, "iRobot's Newest Roomba Uses AI to Avoid Dog Poop."

In this complex system, different types of data, associated with particular activities, are input into different types of AI models. These models then perform a number of tasks that previously would have depended on human intelligence—as well as some new tasks that would not have been possible previously—such as analyzing activities, optimizing operations, applying rules, interacting with customers, and formulating predictions. All of these models are combined in the factory's hybrid model, which interconnects the various tasks performed at the factory and produces outputs—alerts, reports, schedules, customer communications, and simulations of possible futures—to inform decision-making and feed data back into the physical environment. While humans may interact with system outputs, factory processes can become increasingly autonomous. All of this creates a "digital twin" or augmented dimension of the physical factory, which profoundly transforms what a factory is and is able to do.[9] And these automated intelligent systems have a profound impact on us and the world.

In "Anatomy of an AI System," Kate Crawford and Vladan Joler analyze the manufacture and functioning of Amazon's Alexa to show how the stack enabling interactions with it "goes well beyond the multi-layered 'technical stack' of data modeling, hardware, servers and networks." "The full stack reaches much further into capital, labor and nature, and demands an enormous amount of each"; the true scale and "costs of these systems—social, environmental, economic, and political—remain hidden."[10] In *The Atlas of AI*, Crawford further reveals how, "At a fundamental level, AI is technical and social practices, institutions and infrastructures, politics and culture." It is a "massive industrial formation," and "we need to expand our understanding of what is under way in the empires of AI, to see what is at stake, and to make better collective decisions about what should come next."[11] AI systems are much more than technological artifacts. Like Čapek's robots, they are revelatory or apocalyptic figures of our current technological society. As a product of human imagination and intelligence, AI reveals our hopes and fears. And, as we continue to design and develop our increasingly complex technological society, it is important to understand how AI is shaping our imagination as our imagination shapes it.

9. OECD, "OECD Framework for the Classification of AI Systems," 61.
10. Crawford and Joler, "Anatomy of an AI System."
11. Crawford, *Atlas of AI*, 8–9, 21.

INTRODUCTION

AI and the Apocalyptic Imagination

This book explores two phenomena: a new phenomenon, artificial intelligence, and an ancient phenomenon, the apocalyptic imagination. And it aims to show how the latter may help shape the former. Both of these terms have broad and broadening semantic ranges, which are explored throughout this book. John McCarthy created the term "artificial intelligence" in 1955 to describe the project of simulating intelligence with computers. Before then, computers could be programmed to perform a variety of logical operations with data through automated processing. Now, computers can be programmed to program themselves and information processing can be autonomous or self-directed. What is considered "AI" today is contested: it can be extended to any type of automated information processing, such as a calculator or a thermostat, or it can be applied to nothing, since no computational artifact matches—let alone exceeds—all of which human intelligence is capable. For many, human-level or general intelligence is the "holy grail" and "real" goal of AI development.[12] In contemporary usage, AI typically refers to self-learning predictive models, such as a machine learning system that determines the optimal way to heat a house based on the observed behaviors of its inhabitants. Throughout this book, AI is used broadly to refer to automated information processing by computational artifacts.

The "apocalyptic imagination," likewise, can be defined broadly or narrowly. In the broadest sense, an "apocalypse" is a revelation or uncovering of something that is hidden. An imagination that is apocalyptic is open to such disclosures through apocalyptic texts, images, objects, and events. More narrowly, due to the popularity of certain apocalypses that focus on the end of the world, the apocalyptic imagination often focuses on the end of life as we know it. In theology, the apocalyptic imagination seeks to uncover the relationships between divine and human knowledge, heaven and earth, eternity and time, and divine and human action. This "cognitive orientation" includes "a transcendent reality, which defines the cosmos and everything in it, but remains *almost* entirely concealed from observation and beyond the grasp of human intellect." It further involves the realization of good over evil, the revelation of which "gives life meaning and purpose" and inspires the creation of a better world in the future.[13] While

12. Stuart Russell, quoted in Ford, *Architects of Intelligence*, 48.
13. Ditommaso, "Apocalypticism and the Popular Culture," 474. Emphasis added.

5

"apocalyptic imagination" is used broadly in this book, in order to explore and link different visions of anticipated ends, the overarching goal in what follows is to present the apocalyptic imagination as an interpretation of reality that uncovers deeper dimensions of knowledge, space, time, and agency to reveal and help realize a new and hopeful view of the world.

It may not be surprising that AI, developed during hot and cold wars, has been connected with the apocalyptic imagination from the beginning. But that association is largely in a narrow, end-of-the-world-as-we-know-it sense. From a biblical and theological perspective, a richer understanding of the apocalyptic imagination, such as the one found in the book of Revelation or the Apocalypse of John, can help us reflect on the role of AI and shape it. Some argue that we cannot "confidently map AI and robots onto" the biblical apocalyptic vision of new creation, which is represented in the Apocalypse of John by a new heaven, a new earth, and a new city.[14] This book highlights resources within the Christian tradition to map new terrain in connection with the automation of information and intelligence, and it argues that this cartographic work may help us discern how AI may participate in new creation and transform other maps of and plans for AI futures.

New information and communication technologies have been reshaping our lives and the environments in which we live for decades. Klaus Schwab of the World Economic Forum claims we are living through "a revolution that is fundamentally changing the way we live, work, and relate to one another." Schwab labels this the "fourth industrial revolution," which is driven by transformative digital technologies such as big data (i.e., the analysis of large datasets), cloud computing, and AI.[15] More profoundly, the philosopher Luciano Floridi argues we are living through a fourth modern scientific revolution, an "information revolution," in which our dependence on automated information processing by artificial agents is "affecting our sense of self, how we relate to each other, and how we shape and interact with our world."[16] AI is transforming what we do, how we understand ourselves, and what we will become and do.

Within the last ten years, especially following the introduction of Siri in 2011, AI has become a ubiquitous and general-purpose technology—like the steam engine, electricity, and the digital computer—and it is now

14. Wyatt and Williams, "Conclusion," in *Robot Will See You Now*, 233.

15. Schwab, *Fourth Industrial Revolution*, 1.

16. Floridi, *Fourth Revolution*, vi.

a regular part of our daily lives and our social imagination. AI applications show us stuff on websites we may be interested in purchasing, enable us to speak to digital devices to purchase stuff, manage the logistics of getting us stuff, and learn how to show us more stuff we may desire. Other AI systems operating in the world include financial decision-making systems, health monitoring and diagnostic systems, facial and other biological recognition systems, warehouse and police robots, and autonomous vehicles. Often, AI functions in seemingly banal ways, as in the ubiquitous "recommended for you" displays we see constantly on our devices. But AI raises a number of questions about how all the data collected by and for these applications is obtained and used, about the influences the algorithms that drive these systems have on our actions, and about the broader social impacts of complex AI systems that may operate independent of human responsibility and accountability.

In addition to ethical questions about data collection, algorithmic agency, and social justice, the power and potential of AI continues to inspire a range of hopes and fears about the future. AI has been described as "the Second Coming and the Apocalypse at the same time."[17] Some visions of AI are optimistic and utopian, anticipating AI to solve known problems and create a superior form of life. Others are pessimistic and dystopian, expecting AI to exacerbate old problems and create new ones. The most extreme anticipations and anxieties include apocalyptic visions of an earthly paradise, posthuman immortality, and the end of the human species and civilization.

The COVID-19 pandemic became a test for many of our aspirations for AI. Governments, businesses, and research centers looked to various AI technologies to identify useful patterns in data, discover information about the virus, and inform our responses to the pandemic. As demonstrated by an online exhibition called "Technologies of Hope," of one hundred pandemic technologies—from quarantine bracelets to surveillance drones—the hype and haste with which AI was applied during the pandemic revealed many of our hopes and fears.[18] These attempts represented imaginative possibilities, but also the practical limits of AI. Pandemic applications of AI also highlighted ethical concerns about both the perpetuation and the creation of economic, racial, and other inequities. The pandemic was also an information crisis that revealed deep challenges in our current information

17. Brockman, *Possible Minds*, xv.
18. Tactical Tech, "Technologies of Hope."

environment about what we may hope, what we can know, and what we should do. As we shape a post-pandemic world with more sober assessments and ethical visions of AI, it is time, as Ruha Benjamin wrote before the pandemic, "to reimagine what is possible."[19]

The increasing role and power of artificial agents in our lives and world requires us to imagine desirable futures with intelligence automation and reimagine undesirable present realities. Since visions of AI often draw from Jewish and Christian apocalyptic categories and narratives, discussions about AI hopes and fears present an opportunity for a deeper engagement with the apocalyptic imagination as we strive "for another and a juster world."[20] This book explores how the Christian apocalyptic imagination provides a constructive conceptual and narrative framework that can transform how we think about and use AI. This framework can help us view our current information revolution as an information revelation about how AI may participate in new creation and enable us to realize a more hopeful, wiser, and better future.

From Negative to Affirmative Apocalypses

To argue the value of the apocalyptic imagination for AI—AI for AI—a few other theses need to be explored. The first is that our entanglement with information and technology is ancient, and that from the beginning we have been shaping technology as it has been shaping us. The second thesis is that we are living through a unique and transformative moment in history. The first chapter explores our historic and current integration with technology and situates the development of AI within the history of information revolutions. Our current information revolution, connected with information automation, is changing how we understand ourselves and our role in the world. But we have experienced previous information revolutions, and this chapter explores three. The first, which accompanied the emergence of our species, was related to information attention. A second was linked with the development of cities and information agencies. A third occurred with the invention of writing and the creation of information artifacts. These three revolutions—from which we gained powers associated with reflective attention, structural agency, and knowledge augmentation—significantly

19. Benjamin, *Race After Technology*, 1.
20. Du Bois, *Souls of Black Folk*, 418.

advanced human development and enhanced our lives. Moreover, there are corollary spiritual developments related to the emergence of spirituality, religious practices, and anticipatory religions that reveal a deeper significance of each information revolution as well as the limits of human autonomy, autonomous agency, and augmented knowledge.

The third thesis is that we have been digitally naïve for too long, and it is past time to upgrade our understanding and use of the digital information communication technologies that enable automated information processing and intelligence automation. The city is our most ancient complex technology, and it is an important image for understanding the history and future of our technological society. To explore the dynamics shaping our present and emerging relationship with technology, the second chapter explores the city of Las Vegas as an apocalyptic image of our technological society as well as a site of competing technological hopes and fears. The surreal and strange city of Las Vegas challenges our expectations and experiences of reality in a way that is best understood through the apocalyptic imagination. In 2019, hoping to inspire optimistic visions for the future, Amazon held its first public AI event in Las Vegas. Jeff Bezos launched the event with the declaration that we are "at the beginning of a golden age of AI," and the event exhibited impressive examples of AI technologies.[21] Many of these technologies were stress-tested the following year, when the COVID-19 pandemic quickly spread across the globe. Amazon's second public AI event was canceled, much of the world went into lockdown, and many problems with real AI were revealed. To interpret Las Vegas as an apocalyptic image of our current technological society, this chapter focuses on two prophets of the technological city and society: Jacques Ellul and Hunter S. Thompson, who provided important critiques of autonomous systems and social structures near the dawn of the information automation revolution. Although both were inspired by the Apocalypse of John, each failed to see how John's apocalyptic vision finds hope and longing realized in and through the technological city.

The third chapter explores the main thesis of this book: that the apocalyptic imagination is a generative resource that can transform how we think about and use AI, enabling us to discern ways artificial agency may participate in new creation. Based on the work of recent biblical scholars, this chapter introduces—or reintroduces—the apocalyptic imagination that shaped early Jewish and Christian apocalyptic literature. In the Apocalypse

21. Amazon, "We're at the Beginning of a Golden Age of AI."

of John, cities are central in and for the narrative. The Apocalypse includes pastoral letters to seven first-century churches, which address conditions in each church and city, but it also opens up readers' imaginations to the presence of two spiritual cities that are present in every city. One of these cities, most powerfully manifested in the imperial city of Rome, is called Babylon. The Apocalypse announces that this evil city is doomed and falling, and that the good city of God—New Jerusalem—is arriving and will be established permanently. Although initially written for ancient cities, the Apocalypse concerns the destiny of every city—and how new creation is situated in and being realized through them. Technologies, deformative as well as transformative, are included in this narrative. The Apocalypse includes ethical critiques of technologies, strategies for resisting and reforming technologies, and—most importantly—focuses attention on how technology may participate in the realization of the ultimate city. This chapter also explores contemporary technological critiques and forms of activism that share ethical commitments and strategies with the Apocalypse.

The fourth chapter provides a brief history of the apocalyptic imagination, especially in the United States during the twentieth century. It describes changes in theological interpretations of the apocalyptic imagination as well as the emergence of more popular forms of it. The concerns of these forms of the apocalyptic imagination narrowed as AI advanced, and constructive questions about AI and the future were left largely to scientists, industrialists, and technocrats. Considering the Century 21 Exposition—America's Space Age World's Fair, held in Seattle in 1962—this chapter explores many of the technological hopes exhibited by the US government, technology companies, and others at that time. Although early wonders of automation were exhibited and admired, the profound social and technological impacts of these changes were not fully grasped. This was perhaps most evident in the way religion was presented and represented at the fair. Keeping the focus on Seattle, this chapter looks at how this city has been shaped by the industrial technological imagination and the condition of that imagination today—and it argues that we need a knowledge and wisdom revolution to accompany our current industrial revolution. The apocalyptic imagination can help, and this chapter concludes by pointing to possible points of convergence among different views of the apocalyptic imagination to see where shared values might converge.

Chapter five compares perceptions about AI in the first two reports from the One Hundred Year Study on Artificial Intelligence project, published in 2016 and 2021, which reflect a negative turn in assessments about the impact of AI. Supplemented with other recent criticisms of AI, this chapter surveys many of the challenges and opportunities for intelligence automation. Drawing together insights, values, and cautions from this and previous chapters, this chapter introduces an apocalyptic scorecard for assessing real and imagined AI using an integral futures approach. The scorecard connects fundamental questions—about what we may hope, what we can know, and what we must do—with the theological virtues of hope, faith, and love as well as shared commitments to hope, wisdom, and justice. Based on these values, the scorecard assesses AI by asking questions about reflective attention, structural agency, knowledge augmentation, ethical foundations, and reformation.

In chapter six, the apocalyptic scorecard is applied to realistic and imagined AI futures. First, it is used to assess AI presented in the speculative short stories in *AI 2041: Ten Visions for Our Future,* by AI expert Kai-Fu Lee and science fiction writer Chen Qiufan. As constructive and hopeful as these stories are, pointing to important ways human life may be enhanced and ethical issues that need to be addressed, these visions do not address adequately important questions asked in the apocalyptic scorecard. There seem to be no shared social or technological structures for intentionally cultivating attention, caring for human agency, curating knowledge augmentation, or facilitating the creation of ethical foundations or means for reforming systems. Consequently, the transformative potential for intelligence automation largely remains unrealized. Next, the scorecard is used to assess artificial general intelligence (AGI) and artificial superintelligence (ASI) in futures imagined by Max Tegmark in *Life 3.0*, which includes the ethical principles developed by his Future of Life Institute. Tegmark's speculations and ethical principles could be augmented with a more robust apocalyptic imagination and with strategies suggested in the apocalyptic scored. Critiques of all these future scenarios point to what is lacking and needed for a better future enhanced by intelligence automation, including: non-commercialized and secure spaces for cultivating reflective attention; nonprofit agencies that develop structural agency for the common good; and human-focused and human-scaled cultural institutions to advance knowledge augmentation and intelligence automation.

The epilogue concludes with brief reflections on how we might begin to reimagine the present to confront present social and technological challenges. This requires becoming postdigital, which includes wise integration of digital information and communication technologies so they may enhance our lives and world. As an extension of our ancient imaginative drives and desires, intelligence automation can have a role in addressing challenges and creating new opportunities. It may also augment our apocalyptic imagination. The book of Acts, which represents the earliest Christians' reflections and actions as they lived into new creation—into the apocalyptic city into which the church is called—can help us discern how we and AI are participating in that reality now.

Looking backwards toward human origins and forwards toward human futures, this book surveys a lot of ground. It also draws from a variety of disciplines—history, biblical studies, information studies, theology, and others—to interpret the emerging landscape of AI. I recognize this work may be like an early modern map of the world, getting some things wrong and leaving blanks due to insufficient information. As we continue to transform our world into an AI-friendly environment, there is new terrain to explore and form. If this new information environment is to enhance rather than inhibit human intelligence, we must continue to grow in our understanding of and for this new world. I hope other explorers will find what is sketched here helpful, and that better cartographers will correct and improve parts or all of my provisional map. We need many more and better maps for our increasingly complex world.

Beyond the Technological Imagination

Franz Kafka's *The Trial*, written a few years before *R.U.R.* and published a few years after it, presents an inviolable bureaucratic system, with inexplicable ends, which uses people's information to make inscrutable decisions about them without their understanding or participation. The harms, privacy expert Daniel Solve points out, "are bureaucratic ones—indifference, error, abuse, frustration, and lack of transparency and accountability."[22] Kafka, who worked for a time investigating insurance claims and assessing compensation connected with industrial accidents, did not imagine rebellious robots. Rather, he imagined more "terrifying" industrial institutions,

---

22. Quoted in O'Gieblyn, *God, Human, Animal, Machine*, 223.

made by humans operating with an inhuman autonomy[23]—"a cage," as he put it in one of his aphorisms, "in search of a bird."[24]

After reading Blaise Pascal, near the end of the first world war, Kafka wrote his own "*pensées*" about his technological age.[25] These reflections include conclusions about technological civilization, such as: "The fact that the only world is a constructed world takes away hope and gives us certainty."[26] Lewis Mumford articulated something similar in 1934, when he pointed out that "our species became mechanical before machines changed the world." Benjamin Peters brings this sentiment into the present age of automated information processing: "The robots will never take over—that has never been the crisis. Rather, robotic analysis of the future took over our minds and language many decades ago."[27] We must remember that our imagination is not reducible to the techniques and tools it creates; we need more than a technological imagination.

Kafka's *pensées* also include theological claims. In one, he declares: "We are sinful, not only because we have eaten from the Tree of Knowledge, but also because we have not yet eaten of the Tree of Life." In the next, he adds: "We were created to live in Paradise, and Paradise was designed to serve us. Our designation has been changed; we are not told whether this has happened to Paradise as well."[28] In Christian Scripture, there is no return to nor a simple restoration of the paradisiacal garden of Eden seen in Genesis. There is, alternatively, at the end of the Apocalypse of John a city with the tree of life in the center of it.[29] The design of this paradise—the end or goal of what Paul calls "new creation"—looks very different from initial creation.[30] The city, one of humanity's greatest technological achievements, is an image of a technological society. Rather than being abandoned like Babel near the beginning of the biblical narrative or annihilated like the Babylon at the end, the technological city is amplified. As we move through an information revolution driven by increasingly powerful technologies

23. Borges, "Kafka and His Precursors," in *Selected Non-Fictions*, 365.

24. Kafka, *Aphorisms*, 16.

25. See North, *Yield*, 4–5.

26. Kafka, *Aphorisms*, 63.

27. Peters, "How Do We Live Now?," in Mullaney et al., eds., *Your Computer Is on Fire*, 383–84.

28. Kafka, *Aphorisms*, 82, 83.

29. See Rev 22:1–2.

30. 2 Cor 5:17.

such as AI, the city of the Apocalypse is an important resource for imagining how our technological innovations may participate in a greater new creation.

1

||||||||||||||||||||||

Information Revolutions
and Revelations

"Science," Luciano Floridi points out, "changes our understanding in two fundamental ways." The discovery of new information can change how we think about the world, but it can also change how we think about ourselves. When scientific discoveries significantly change both our self-understanding and our understanding of the world, Floridi argues, we can speak of a major scientific revolution. While our present information age and society has ancient roots, Floridi argues that the current digital transformation of our lives and world constitutes a revolution.[1]

Floridi identifies four major scientific revolutions that have transformed our understanding of ourselves and our world during the modern era. The first followed the printing of Nicolaus Copernicus's *On the Revolutions of the Celestial Spheres* in 1543, which placed the sun at the center of his model of the universe. This heliocentric view of the world literally displaced both the earth and humanity from the center of the cosmos, requiring us to reimagine our place in it. The second revolution followed Charles Darwin's 1859 publication of *On the Origin of Species*. Darwin's explanation of natural selection, which radically altered understandings of human origins and biological adaptation, required us to reimagine our place in the biological world. Following Sigmund Freud, whose work in psychological analysis complicated more rationalistic views of the mind, a

---

1. Floridi, *Fourth Revolution*, 87.

third revolution changed how we understood minds, feelings, intelligence, and consciousness.[2]

Within the last one hundred years, we created technologies for automated information processing. Within the last fifty years, our intelligent technologies became digital, globally networked, and mobile. The creation and proliferation of increasingly complex information processing technologies and our interactions with them are having a significant impact on us and our reality, and Floridi argues we are experiencing an information revolution. This revolution is revealing the importance of information in shaping us and our world, which casts "new light on who we are and how we are related to the world."[3] Information and communication technologies have changed both how we interpret and how we design the world. "Smart and autonomous agents no longer need to be human," Floridi observes, and we are shaping a world that is increasingly "friendly" or accommodating to artificial agents.[4] In Floridi's words, we are beginning to understand ourselves as information organisms ("inforgs") living in an information environment ("infosphere"). Being an inforg is not about extending ourselves with tools or integrating technologies into ourselves as cyborgs—we have been doing these things for some time. Nor is it about transforming ourselves into something more than human, which remains speculative. Being an inforg means seeing ourselves as inhabiting an environment that is being shaped for and shaping both natural and artificial informational agents.[5]

As with previous scientific revolutions, we have gained new concepts and insights that enhance our understanding of the reality of information, not only presently but throughout natural and human history. From an informational perspective, at least three previous major information revolutions can be identified that have shaped human history. The first, connected with the emergence of our species, enabled us to process information imaginatively and reflectively. A second, linked with the development of cities, came with the creation of information agencies to realize shared goals. A third, following the invention of writing, came with the creation of information artifacts to augment the discovery and sharing of knowledge. Each of these information revolutions significantly enhanced human abilities

2. See Floridi, *Fourth Revolution*, 87–94

3. Floridi, "Why Information Matters," 14.

4. Floridi, *Fourth Revolution*, 32, 40.

5. See Floridi, *Fourth Revolution*, esp. 94–96.

and agency, and also revealed new insights about what a human being is and about our role in the universe. These insights can help us navigate our current revolution related to information automation, which enables the automation of intelligence.

The First Information Revolution: Attention

The history of human technology began about three million years ago with rocks. Sharp flakes, initially created through natural processes, were collected by early hominins and used as tools for cutting food. At some point hominins began creating sharp flakes themselves, deliberately hammering rocks together; about one million years ago, they were hammering stones into teardrop-shaped hand axes. These lithic tools could be used to crack open and get at the marrow of bones of animals already killed and picked over by larger predators. Able to access richer sources of calories from larger animals they could not yet hunt themselves, ancient humans began ascending the food chain and achieved other physical, social, and cultural advances—such as larger brains and more complex technological developments.[6]

The existence of early lithic technologies represents the emergence of mental and motor skills capable of purposely manipulating raw materials and transforming them into reusable tools.[7] These tools functioned as a new interface with the environment and as a means of extending control over it.[8] They became an extension of hominins and materially communicated what was possible with tools, "eventually leading to the establishment of humans as the most successful tool users on the planet."[9] By a million years ago, Nigel Shadbolt and Roger Hampson point out, technology became "a central catalyst for our biology" and ever since our biology "has been remaking our technology."[10] The emergence of technological creativity was a significant event for our lineage's physical evolution and cultural development, as

---

6. See Plummer and Finestone, *Rethinking Human Evolution*, 267. Older evidence for lithic technology may extend back to 3.3 million years ago. See 268.

7. See Suddendorf and Dong, "On the Evolution of Imagination and Design," 457, 463.

8. See Fragaszy et al., "Fourth Dimension of Tool Use."

9. Biro et al., "Tool Use as Adaptation."

10. Shadbolt and Hampson, *Digital Ape*, 13.

technological developments "codirected human evolution."[11] As Ron Cole-Turner points out, "Before we became humans, we made tools. And almost immediately, our tools began to make us more and more human."[12]

After the control and daily use of fire some 300,000 years ago—used for cooking, light, warmth, weapons, and clearing land—ancient human artificial agency, aided by tools and associated techniques, began to outpace earlier natural forms of agency. Moreover, human biology became dependent on the objects used to amplify capacities—such as fire for digestible food, clothing in the absence of fur, and shelters for new environments.[13] Human technological development merged with natural evolution in such a way that, as John Durham Peters explains, questions of how to define nature, humans, and technology becomes the same question: "We know and use nature only though the artifacts we make—both out of nature and out of our own bodies—and these artifacts can enter into nature's own history."[14]

The emergence of *Homo sapiens*, beginning after 200,000 years ago and complete by 60,000 years ago, was accompanied with an explosion of technologies for personal ornamentation, art, elaborate burials, complex multicomponent weaponry, long-distance trade, time-keeping, and scheduling. These artifacts are evidence of enhanced working memory, abstract reasoning, conceptual self-awareness, symbolic thinking, grammatical language, and instruction[15]—and of the first major information revolution, when humans developed a new capability for information attention. Information, defined as well-structured and meaningful data, exists throughout nature.[16] The earliest forms of life evolved as reflexive data processing agents, collecting environmental data through natural sensors and then reacting to survive. But *Homo sapiens*, with and through their ancient technologies, became dis-automatized from this instinctive data-seeking drive. We became the first known species to reflect on the meaning of data and to perceive and understand information. Information preceded us, but *Homo*

11. Plummer and Finestone, *Rethinking Human Evolution*, 267–68.

12. Cole-Turner, *End of Adam and Eve*, 54.

13. See Shadbolt and Hampson, *Digital Ape*, 85.

14. Peters, *Marvelous Clouds*, 51.

15. See Coolidge and Wynn, *Rise of Homo Sapiens*, 5–6.

16. "Data" can be defined as "entities used as evidence of a phenomenon for a particular purpose." Darch, "Data Ethics," 77.

sapiens crossed a semantic threshold and were able to understand it was there.

Seeking and sharing discovered information became a defining characteristic of our species. With the ability to think about information abstractly and reflectively, instead of reflexively and automatically, humans were able to comprehend and communicate information—as well as disinformation and misinformation—about observed phenomena, the minds of others, unobserved phenomena, and creative possibilities. Reflective attention created new symbolic mental worlds that enabled humans to explore, transcend, and change reality by imagining alternatives to actual past and present experiences. They could anticipate and plan for the future, develop innovative plans, stories, social systems, and new environments, and contemplate what followed death.[17] Through attention, humans extended themselves beyond their initial present conditions and became receptive to new understandings of themselves and the world. They also imagined and engaged in rituals to encounter a deeper spiritual dimension to reality.[18]

The ability to develop aspirational goals and desires over more basic demands and drives is not easily maintained. As Adam Gazzaley and Larry Rosen explain in *The Distracted Mind: Ancient Brains in a High-Tech World*, "the very essence of what has evolved furthest in our brains to make us human—our ability to set high-level goals for ourselves—collides headfirst with our brains' fundamental limitations in cognitive control: attention, working memory, and goal management." This imbalance between aspirational goals and cognitive limits, they conclude, remains "a fundamental vulnerability."[19] To leverage information attention, humans needed—and still need—to develop social and technological structures to sustain and augment attention.

Interestingly, in *Sapiens: A Brief History of Humankind*, Yuval Harari calls this moment in human evolutionary history the "Tree of Knowledge mutation."[20] The tree of knowledge is one of the trees God grows in the pleasant and cultivated garden of Eden, situated in the midst of it with the tree of life (Gen 2:9). God places the first human in the garden "to till [or work] it and keep it," permitting consumption of fruit from every tree

17. See Taylor, "Transcending Time, Place, and/or Circumstance," 3.

18. See Haught, *New Cosmic Story*, 9.

19. Gazzaley and Rosen, *Distracted Mind*, xiv, 3.

20. Harari, *Sapiens*, 21.

except from "the tree of the knowledge of good and evil" (2:15, 17).[21] That fruit, God says, leads to death. God's gift of a garden includes a present danger, and it is connected with the pursuit of knowledge. The narrative does not seem interested in explaining the origin of or justification for this existential risk, but Walter Brueggemann observes that it is an important statement about human anthropology: humans are defined by "vocation, permission, and prohibition." Human destiny concerns the balance of these three characteristics—a balance of commission and constraint—which humans fail to maintain from the beginning.[22]

Before this failure is realized, the first humans are drawn into the first theological discussion in the Hebrew Bible by the shrewdest animal God had made—the serpent. The serpent misquotes God: the permission "you may freely eat of every tree of the garden, but of the tree of the knowledge of good and evil you shall not eat, for in the day that you eat of it you shall die" becomes "you shall not eat from any tree in the garden" (2:16–17; 3:1). The woman corrects the serpent—"We may eat of the fruit of the trees in the garden"—but adds to God's prohibition: "nor shall you touch it" (3:2–3). The serpent says instead of death their "eyes will be opened" and they "will be like God, knowing good and evil" (3:5). The humans, desiring the promise of knowledge independent of God, take and eat the fruit. Immediately, as the serpent promised, "the eyes of both were opened" (3:7). They gain knowledge of their nakedness, they become afraid of God, and they are expelled from the garden so they may not eat also from the tree of life—which was not previously prohibited, and will not be found again until it arrives with New Jerusalem (Rev 22:2). Through a clever language game, which turns God and God's instructions into abstractions, a relationship of trust is disrupted. A prohibition is reframed as a possibility, and death comes to dominate the biblical narrative (see Rom 5:12). Inverting the message that "There is no fear in love, but perfect love casts out fear" (1 John 4:18), Brueggemann points out, they learn that "Perfect fear casts out love."[23]

Before they are displaced east of Eden, God makes and gives Adam and Eve clothes and they retain the vocation given at the beginning of Genesis (Gen 2:15; 3:23). This work will be performed with the knowledge of an alternative to the reality of evil and short days: there is the possibility and promise of a greater good and life. Intelligence can be defined as "the

21. Unless indicated otherwise, translations are from the NRSV.
22. Brueggemann, *Genesis*, 46.
23. Brueggemann, *Genesis*, 53.

capacity to do the right thing at the right time, in a context where doing nothing (making no change in behavior) would be worse."[24] For humans, what is right becomes a moral question and the ongoing pursuit and application of knowledge now requires wisdom to discern what is true and good from what is false and bad, and to distinguish between what we *can* know and do from what we *may* know and *must* do. This begins with discovering and reflecting on information. When information that is relevant and may be accounted for is understood, information may be upgraded to knowledge.[25] Knowledge possesses potential, and when it takes the form of specialized understanding or technical skills—when it is linked with a practical concern about how to do something—it can be called wisdom. These concepts are fluid and overlap, but they point to the sophisticated dynamics of human intelligence that are manifested through understanding, communication, action, and judgment. As Jesus said, "Wisdom is justified by her works" (Matt 11:19 ASV).

In Exodus, for example, God's instructions for the construction of the tabernacle and its furnishings are followed by a description of Bezalel as someone with "ability [or wisdom], intelligence [or understanding], and knowledge in every kind of craft, to devise artistic designs, to work in gold, silver, and bronze, in cutting stones for setting, and in carving wood, in every kind of craft" (31:1–5). Specialized and technical forms of wisdom, however, are not sufficient for right or just relationships in life. In Ezekiel, the ruler of Tyre is praised for being "wiser than Daniel": By "great wisdom in trade," the prophet declares, Tyre amassed and increased its wealth (28:3, 5). But, Ezekiel says, the fullness of wisdom and perfection of beauty given in Eden was corrupted by "the unrighteousness of [their] trade," which was characterized by pride and violence (28:18). Full wisdom includes both practical and moral agency. Thus in Deuteronomy, Moses tells the Israelites to keep God's commandments so they will live and be known as "a wise and discerning (or understanding) people" (4:6). In the legend of the fall is an acknowledgment that human intelligence—finding meaning in data, knowledge in information, and wisdom in knowledge—cannot nor should be autonomous. Knowing and doing what is right, the prophet Micah reminds, depends on walking humbly with God: acting in a careful and just way that attends to God's wisdom and love (6:8).

24. Bryson, "Past Decade and Future of AI's Impact on Society," 129.
25. See Floridi, *Philosophy of Information*, 267–68.

A Second Information Revolution: Agencies

Some 12,000 years ago, humans "began to devote almost all their time and effort to manipulating the lives of a few animal and plant species" to provide supplies of food, raw materials, and muscle power. Clearing forests and fields, digging canals and ploughing furrows, building houses and walls, humans became adept at creating artificial environments within natural ones. These increasingly complex artificial environments, which required more sophisticated social structures for organizing rules, trade, and cultural activities, resulted in one of the most significant technological innovations of our species: cities.[26]

The earliest cities were organized many millennia ago, independently in Asia and Europe, in Africa, and in both Americas. Around the planet, Greg Woolf argues, local consensus emerged recurrently "about civic values, including the value of living in a city," and cities became a distinct feature of human development.[27] Cities comprised a set of technologies that provided stability, security, economies of scale, new opportunities for specialization, and the creation of cultural goods. At the same time, cities created new social hierarchies and inequalities, food insecurity and disease, and more impersonal relationships. And, often with devastating effects, they permanently altered physical environments. Nevertheless, over the following millennia, cities become "a central part of the experience of the human species, and cities have become one of our species' favored niches."[28]

Complex, shared, and future-oriented goals—overcoming the limitations of individual intelligence—were realized through information agencies. This second information revolution involved political, economic, religious, and other institutions organizing laws for courts, accounting for markets, narratives for temples, and instructions for other collaborative processes to structure and sustain civic life. Aggregating attention and agency, these cultural information agencies created a structural agency that enabled cities to operate as multi-agent and semiautonomous systems to extend collective human actions across space and time.

Although often viewed as a more natural environment, the garden of Eden presumes the presence of agricultural activity. The first human was a "tiller of the earth" and so was his first son, Cain (Gen 4:2). Cain's brother,

---

26. Harari, *Sapiens*, 77–97.
27. Woolf, *Life and Death of Ancient Cities*, 310.
28. Woolf, *Life and Death of Ancient Cities*, xiii.

the second son Abel, had a different agricultural occupation: keeping sheep. After Cain killed Abel, mixing his blood with the ground, he found a second vocation in urban design. He named the first city after his son Enoch, and both Enochs can be seen as fulfillments of the mandate to fill and rule the earth, to procreate and create (Gen 1:28). From Cain's line comes the creation of music and metalworking, which enrich human culture and city life.[29] However, urban cultures seem to be "dispreferred" in Genesis.[30] Indeed, at the narrative nadir of Genesis, immediately before the calling of Abram, is the story of Babel. Migrants come together and use their technology to transform natural materials into bricks and mortar in order to build a city. They say, "Come, let us build ourselves a city, and a tower with its top in the heavens, and let us make a name for ourselves; otherwise we shall be scattered abroad upon the face of the whole earth" (11:4).

The imagined city promises to be a place where, together, people may be freed from the migratory challenges of securing food, shelter, and safety—a place of thriving permanence instead of precarious survival. But, as the Tower of Babel rises into the heavens, God comes down to see this technological wonder. God is impressed, and says, "This is only the beginning of what they will do; nothing that they propose to do will now be impossible for them" (11:6). God then confuses the one people's language, disrupting shared understanding, communication, trust, and community. This halts their creative work, and their fears of being scattered are realized.

The Babel narrative is often read as a straightforward critique of urban culture and technology, but the sins of Babel's builders are unnamed. Their actions do, however, reflect those of the inhabitants of Eden. According to Brueggemann, the pattern repeated at Babel is one of "self-sufficiency and autonomy." Freedom is constrained by a fear that seeks an independent form of certainty, "a fortress mentality," which "seeks to survive by its own resources."[31] Rather than a critique of cities or technology per se, the narrative of Babel is a critique of self-securing and self-serving autonomy. Alluding to the seat of the ancient Babylonian empire, Babel also can be read as a critique of imperial autonomy—the creation of independent systems and structures for oppressive autonomous agency.

Without an absolute condemnation of the city, the possibility of an alternative faithful city remains open. The admonition about autonomous

29. See Gen 4:17–22; and Provan, *Discovering Genesis*, 103.

30. Ando, "Children of Cain," 52.

31. Brueggemann, *Genesis*, 46, 100.

systems endures, but the ruins of Babel signify that structural agency depends on more than itself. Human attention and agency can be empowered for good ends through shared structural agency, but human power over structural powers needs to be maintained carefully—or the power of autonomous systems will overwhelm it, become oppressive, and ultimately collapse. Fyodor Dostoevsky, for example, described the Crystal Palace— the building in London in which the technological accomplishments of the Industrial Revolution were exhibited in 1851 at the first world exhibition, the "Great Exhibition of the Industry of All Nations"—"as an apocalyptic nightmare of a sort of the Tower of Babel." There, he wrote, the "masses saw escape from the rigid oppression, in the name of utopia on earth, by a mechanical, all-pervasive system."[32] What the masses saw, though, were new technologies over which they had little power and that would be used to oppress them in new ways.

A Third Information Revolution: Artifacts

A third information revolution occurred some 5,000 years ago, when information agencies developed written communication and information artifacts. By the third millennium BCE, in Sumerian cities in southern Mesopotamia, mnemonic pictographic symbols evolved into a coded system of wedge-shaped marks called cuneiform, the earliest known form of writing.[33] Administrative and literary texts were inscribed on stone and clay tablets, initially to manage the present affairs of cities but increasingly to reflect on "a deep past and a far future."[34] Time, as Augustine observes, is experienced through memories of the past, expectations about the future, and direct perceptions of the present—all of which are held together by the "faculty of attention."[35] Material texts were created to communicate a fuller experience of temporality throughout expanding communities and across generations, as well as with divine entities. Religion, like other human cultural activities, was now mediated through information artifacts. And because an information artifact cannot be "fully subject to the instrumental

---

32. Quoted in Provan, *Discovering Genesis*, 130.
33. See Suarez and Woudhuysen, eds., *Book*, 3–5.
34. Woolf, *Life and Death of Ancient Cities*, 53.
35. Augustine, *Confessions*, 269, 278.

intentions of its users," as Jeremy Stolow says, it was seen as participating "in the realm of the transcendent."[36]

To preserve information from being lost, and provide immediate and long-term access to communications inscribed in records and books, information and attention management structures and systems—such as archives and libraries—joined other urban institutions by the second millennium BCE.[37] Initially technologies of and for kingdoms and empires, ancient archives and libraries adopted three main functions to preserve memories of the past, anticipations of the future, and add to these through the creation of new knowledge in the present. First, they determined to represent a particular culture through fixed expression of knowledge. This intention led to the selection of texts judged worthy of attention. Access to these texts was then mediated through social and technological systems for acquisition, classification, retrieval, dissemination, storage, and preservation.[38] Through this curatorial work, libraries and similar institutions became a technology for knowledge augmentation by creating models of structural agency for individual and collective information agency.

In the ancient world, the political and intellectual power and possibility of the library for knowledge augmentation was most significantly manifested in—and lived on through the myth of—the Library of Alexandria. Alexander the Great's successors in Egypt, the Ptolemies, established a library to collect, "if possible, all the books in the world," in order to control—intellectually, at least—the world.[39] Their library, supporting an institution for scholarly inquiry and production (the *mouseîon*), made Alexandria a significant cultural center in the Hellenistic world during the reign of the Ptolemies. The Library of Alexandria fell into oblivion, but its legend created the future-shaping ideal of the library as a place "where knowledge could be created."[40]

As knowledge was being augmented through information artifacts during the last few centuries before the Common Era, new religious and philosophical approaches to wisdom emerged throughout the ancient

36. Stolow, quoted in Supp-Montgomerie, *When the Medium Was the Mission*, 9.

37. See Valentine, *Social History of Books and Libraries*, 26–29.

38. See Ryholt and Barjamovic, eds., *Libraries before Alexandria*. For the presence of these three main functions in ancient libraries, see Too, *Idea of the Library in the Ancient World*, 4–5, 175, 188, 242–43.

39. Letter of Aristeas, 12.

40. Ovenden, *Burning the Books*, 44.

world in Greece, Judea, Persia, China, India, and elsewhere. Karl Jaspers called this a pivotal or "axial age," marking a shift in attention toward deeper questions about ultimate realities. John Haught says, "What was occurring during the axial period—and continues now—was the birth of a new sense of rightness . . . sharper distinctions than ever before between a right way and a wrong way to live, think, act, work, and pray." Haught describes these approaches to wisdom as anticipatory, seeking "redemptive rightness and revelatory fullness . . . by expectancy rather than mere recovery." Haught's "way of anticipation" looks toward the future fulfillment of the universe, the end or goal—*telos*—of its narrative.[41] Beyond the fleeting, fragmentary, and fraught present, anticipatory religions expect something more permanent, unified, and right through faith, which Haught describes as "the experience of being grasped by 'that which is to come.' . . . the 'future' that comes to meet us, takes hold of us, and makes us new."[42]

This teleologically-grounded view of the future does not simply view the future as a product of what has preceded it, an outcome "driven from behind" by the past and present. What Haught describes is an understanding of the future that is "driven by what is ahead"—a future that "describes what is coming" and "speaks of arrival." This alternative way of viewing the future, Michael Burdett argues, "can provide a more robust account of the future." When it "emphasizes the themes of possibility and promise," it can provide corrective narratives and/or counternarratives: "The future does not just depend upon the present actuality but upon a robust account of possibility which does not define possibility according to the actual."[43]

The apocalyptic imagination emerged as one way of exploring how rightness could be realized in and from the future—especially when so much was wrong in the present. A confluence of Jewish as well as Babylonian, Persian, and Hellenistic influences, the apocalyptic imagination seeks an uncovering of a hidden or deeper reality that leads to the "end of the ongoing struggle between good and evil in history."[44] Apocalyptic thinking is often expressed through literary works called apocalypses, although it can be found in others genres. A widely accepted definition, developed in the 1970s, describes an apocalypse as

41. Haught, *New Cosmic Story*, 11, 23, 35.
42. Haught, *God after Darwin*, 97.
43. Burdett, *Eschatology and the Technological Future*, 2–3, 237.
44. Collins, "General Introduction," in *Encyclopedia of Apocalypticism, Volume I*, vii.

a genre of revelatory literature with a narrative framework, in which a revelation is mediated by an otherworldly being to a human recipient, disclosing a transcendent reality which is both temporal, insofar as it envisages eschatological salvation, and spatial insofar as is involves another, supernatural world.[45]

Jewish prophets had been declaring "the end" as early the eighth century BCE, but these were local, near, and this-worldly ends. When Amos announced "the end," it concerned the fall of the northern kingdom of Israel to Assyria (8:2). But by the end of the Babylonian exile in the sixth century BCE, "the end" became more cosmic and distant. Prophecies also extended into the age or life to come. The new creation imagined in Isaiah 56–66, for example, is eschatological—i.e., concerned with last (*eschatos*) things—but it is "oriented toward a restored earthly society."[46] Daniel 7–12, however, "written in the heat of persecution" under Seleucid rule in Judea in the second century BCE, explores a spatial and temporal transcendent reality that parallels human experience and is "on a collision course with history."[47] King Nebuchadnezzar of Babylon, along with all of his imperial successors, is only provisionally "king of kings" (2:37).

The earliest Christians were inspired by Jewish apocalyptic images, concepts, and narratives about a new and better world. As Adela Yarbro Collins states, apocalyptic thinking "is the primary source of the narratives and symbolic systems that inspired John the Baptist, Jesus, the earliest community after Easter, and Paul."[48] The resurrection of Jesus was understood as an apocalyptic event, which began a hoped-for transformation of the world. According to N. T. Wright, the Christian apocalyptic imagination opened "up a vision of new creation which precisely overlaps with, and radically transforms, the present creation."[49]

Apocalyptic literature is a "scribal phenomenon," typically composed by those who have extensive knowledge of literary sources and textual traditions.[50] Written to reveal what is hidden, apocalyptic texts often feature textual artifacts—such as books in the form of scrolls (*biblia*)—within

45. Collins, *Apocalyptic Imagination*, 5.

46. Collins, "From Prophecy to Apocalypticism: The Expectation of the End," in *Encyclopedia of Apocalypticism, Volume I*, 134.

47. Collins, *Apocalyptic Imagination*, 47; Cook, "Apocalyptic Prophecy," 20.

48. Yarbro Collins, "Apocalypticism and Christian Origins," 338.

49. Wright, *History and Eschatology*, 156.

50. Collins, *Apocalyptic Imagination*, 47.

their narratives to facilitate disclosures of information. In the first-century Apocalypse of John, John says he was directed to "write in a [scroll: *biblion*] what you see and send it to the seven churches" in Asia Minor (1:11). After writing seven letters to the seven churches, John writes about a vision of "a scroll written on the inside and on the back, sealed with seven seals" (5:1). The narrative advances as the seals are broken, and other visions follow. Before the visions associated with the seven seals end, John is told to stop writing and he sees another scroll, which he is told to eat (10:8–10). The visions continue, and at the final judgment more scrolls are opened. These are books representing works, and people are "judged according to their works, as recorded in the [scrolls]" (20:12; cp. Dan 7:10). But there is also the "book of life," representing grace, in which names were "written from the foundation of the world" (13:8; cp. Dan 12:1).[51] Books are both metaphors for and means of apocalypse.

Although the Gospel of John is not often read as an apocalyptic text, John Ashton argues that it has an "affinity" with apocalyptic literature and "may be called an apocalypse in reverse."[52] All the dualisms the apocalyptic imagination seeks to resolve—questions about how divine knowledge, agency, space, and time relate to human understanding and action, the world, and history—are fully collapsed in the person and work of Jesus within John's narrative. He is the otherworldly being, the word and wisdom of God who was in the beginning with God, who became flesh and mediated a revelation about God's love to the world (1:1–14; cp. 1 Cor 1:24). Jesus disclosed a transcendent temporal and spatial reality by descending from heaven and providing eternal life (3:16, 31). And, in a more traditionally apocalyptic manner, he claims the apocalyptic title "Son of Man"—who appears in the apocalyptic text Daniel 7:13—and speaks of a future resurrection (5:27–29). Jesus claims that he himself is the resurrection and the life, and he is raised from the dead (11:25). If a book is both a message and a material medium, Jesus is like an incarnate apocalyptic text.

The conclusion of John declares that information artifacts participate in God's apocalyptic work of augmenting knowledge. One ending says: "these [signs] are written so that you may come [or continue] to believe that Jesus is the Messiah [Christ], the Son of God, and that through believing you may have life in his name" (20:30–31). The other ending, echoing Ecclesiastes's statement that there is no end to the making of many books

---

51. See Blount, *Revelation*, 374.

52. Ashton, *Gospel of John and Christian Origins*, 97, 118.

(12:12), acknowledges the importance of selection. Eugene Peterson's translation in *The Message* reads: "There are so many other things Jesus did. If they were all written down, each of them, one by one, I can't imagine a world big enough to hold such a library of books" (21:25).[53]

Christian Artificial Agency

Christians quickly became creators and collectors of books. In addition to Jewish books, which had been formative for Jesus and his earliest witnesses, followers of Jesus created texts about his teachings and life. These circulated among churches, and church leaders developed lists of texts worthy of being read in churches as well as creeds for interpreting these texts. Taking advantage of resources for knowledge production in important imperial cities—including a thriving commercial book industry, an abundance of libraries, competing textual communities, and schools of instruction[54]—Christians created new types of books, creative forms of textual scholarship, and began building their own libraries. Christians advanced the use of the codex, a technique previously used to bind together reusable wax tablets, which could be used to hold together longer and more texts than a scroll could include. Codices also could keep together more complex texts, such as Origen's *Hexapla*. This six-column layout of Hebrew and Greek texts helped establish the text of the Christian Old Testament, and provided a methodology for creating critical editions of texts. A codex functioned as a book repository or library (*bibliotheca*).[55]

By the fourth century, Christians began to connect faith with physical places such as cathedrals, sacred sites, and cities. Soon after Constantine's edict of toleration, a grand cathedral at Tyre was completed. In praising its structure and significance, Eusebius of Caesarea was among the first Christians to speak of a building's ability to create and increase faith—an agency previously preserved for God, individuals, communities, and oral and written texts. Church buildings "replaced the agora as the main locus of urban life and local civic identity" in many imperial cities, and they became "central hubs of the urban network and dominate[d] urban infrastructure."[56]

53. Peterson, *Message*, 239.
54. See Wendt, "Intellectualizing Religion in the Cities," 102, 118.
55. See Grafton and Williams, *Christianity and the Transformation of the Book*.
56. Blömer, "Sacred Spaces and New Cities in the Byzantine East," 214.

In the centuries that followed, the church building "became the definitive locus and symbol of Christianity." And it became common to think of faith "as taking place in some type of city, and the city as a natural, even the natural environment for faith."[57]

It took hundreds of years for Christianity to leverage the gains of the first three information revolutions, but Christians developed creeds for reflective attention, church institutions for structural agency, and libraries for knowledge augmentation. In the early twelfth century, Hugh of St. Victor articulated a theology of technology that recognized the divine use of human artificial agency. Hugh identified three "books" of creation. One book reveals God's work of initial creation "in the beginning," which formed the world out of nothing and established the subsequent work of nature: "let the earth put forth . . ." (Gen 1:1, 11). A second book reveals the work of humans, which is made out of something and adds to nature: "the work of the artificer is to put together things disjoined or to disjoin those put together . . . 'they sewed fig leaves together and made loincloths for themselves'" (Gen 3:7).[58] But human work is revealed as corruptible, deforming relationships with God, nature, other humans, human creations, and our own selves. This requires another book to reveal "the Wisdom by which God made all his works."[59] The third book of creation is the work of Christ, which includes his life, Scripture, the sacraments, and the communities that represent Christ.[60] Mediated through embodied, textual, and ecclesial forms, this work takes up and transforms all work into new creation.

Hugh claimed the uniqueness of human nature includes the power to imagine what is not present, to communicate this information, and to transform understanding into action.[61] When imagination and information result in the contemplation of truth, and when actions are virtuous, we participate in wisdom and Christ himself.[62] For Hugh, technology— or, more specifically, the medieval "mechanical arts," divided into "fabric making, armament, commerce, agriculture, hunting, medicine, and theatrics"—has a central role in reforming our relationship with God, nature,

---

57. Morgan, "Faith and the City in the 4th Century CE," 71, 80, 91–92.

58. Hugh of St. Victor, *Didascalicon*, 55.

59. Hugh, quoted in Illich, *In the Vineyard of the Text*, 124.

60. See Coolman, *Theology of Hugh of St. Victor*, 131, 170.

61. See Hugh, *Didascalicon*, 50.

62. See Hugh, *Didascalicon*, 54–55, 74; Coolman, *Theology of Hugh of St. Victor*, 21.

and others.[63] Books and libraries, along with other technologies of learning, can be added to Hugh's list of technologies for wisdom and love.[64] For Hugh, technology is "part of the human quest for wisdom"; it extends our abilities and understanding; and, when used wisely, it can reform what has been deformed.[65] Technology may be understood as part of Christ's work of new creation, reconciling divine, natural, and human artificial creativity.

Hugh's theological affirmation of technology clearly emphasized and highlighted tools and techniques that already had been integrated into human history with the development and growth of Christianity. In the centuries following Hugh, Christianity remained associated with libraries, creeds, and institutions, but new urban institutions began to rival monastic literacy and libraries—especially universities in cities such as Bologna, Paris, and Oxford, which trained clergyman but also noblemen and merchants. The printing press—"the blueprint of all mechanization to follow," according to Marshal McLuhan—mass-produced different versions of the Bible, indulgences and Reformation tracts, and books that challenged old orthodoxies and institutions.[66] Creedal disputes involved new nations and gunpowder, and the compass expanded the geographical reach of Christian agencies as "the deepest reality of the Christian social imagination" was being thwarted as it was "woven into processes of colonial dominance."[67] At the same time, literacy and learning—initially advanced to facilitate access to and use of sacred texts—continued to increase along with the availability of books.

Growth in knowledge and wisdom was far from direct or perfect, but early modern thinkers such as Francis Bacon continued to propose new methods for further augmenting human intelligence and agency. Bacon, who advocated for studying both "the book of God's word" and "the book of God's works," proposed more scientific methods for advancing knowledge that overcame flawed faculties, limited perspectives and experiences, and received dogmas and superstitions.[68] In a seventeenth-century "fable" titled *New Atlantis*, Bacon imagined a society dedicated to scientific discovery, technological innovation, and theological reflection. The discovery

63. Hugh, *Didascalicon*, 74.

64. See Hugh, *Didascalicon*, 105, 115, 118.

65. Allen, *Spiritual Theology*, 119.

66. McLuhan, *Essential McLuhan*, 244.

67. Jennings, *Christian Imagination*, 6, 8.

68. Bacon, *Advancement of Learning*, 22.

of this island, Bensalem (which could be translated as "son of [Jeru]salem or peace," is allusively introduced as a realization of new creation: "as in the beginning . . . [God] would now discover land to us, that we might not perish." About twenty years after the ascension of Christ, the Bensalemites had received "all the canonical books of the Old and New Testament . . . and the Apocalypse itself." At the center of Bacon's ideal society is Salomon's House—with massive and diverse facilities for studying natural phenomena and creating artificial works, as well as places for honoring human inventors and God—which functions to understand the world, enlarge "the bounds of Human Empire," and to effect "all things possible."[69] In Bacon's view, the ultimate transformation of the world remained the work of God. New Atlantis is not New Jerusalem; it is rather a significant realization of it, showing how humans may participate in transforming the world through their work and works. As Burdett observes, "The ultimate future is also a product of our human work today."[70]

The Industrial Revolution

By the seventeenth century, an "engine" increasingly referred less to "a tool, implement, or simple mechanical device" and more often to "a complicated machine with moving parts, for producing a given physical effect, especially the conversion of power into motion."[71] A simple tool such as an axe or a plough is a "first-order" technology: it is an artifact used to interact with the environment. When a technology is inserted between humans and another technology, such as the movable type used in a printing press, it is a "second-order" technology. The second-order technology of portable steam and electric engines that provide energy to other technologies marked the arrival of the Industrial Revolution. An industrial city became "a noisy world of gears, clocks, shafts, wheels, and powered mechanisms, characterized not just by the humanity–technology–nature relation but, more significantly, by the humanity–technology–technology relation." "Modernity," Floridi observes, became "a world of complex and networked dependencies, of mechanical chain-reactions as well as locked-in connections: no trains without railways and coal, no cars without petrol

69. Bacon, *New Atlantis*, 152, 159–60, 177.

70. Burdett, *Eschatology and the Technological Future*, 15.

71. *Oxford English Dictionary* (2000), s.v. "engine."

stationseand oil, and so forth, in a mutually reinforcing cycle that is both robust and constraining."[72]

During the latter half of the nineteenth century, technology became "a vast matrix of elements": machines (such as telegraphs and trains); expertise (coding and engineering); raw materials and infrastructures (telegraph cables and railroad tracks); conventions (forms and schedules); cultures (communication and travel); and political systems (nationalism and colonialism).[73] But what was happening to the place of humans as the new technological culture of industrial societies advanced? Dostoevsky, through the unnamed antihero in *Notes from Underground*, offered one critique in the 1860s. A former bureaucrat at a civil information agency, in the "abstract and intentional city" of St. Petersburg, now living underground questions the methodology and metrics of his aspiring industrial society. Can human potential be realized fully through science and technology? If so, "all that is needed is to discover the laws of nature," classify and calculate all human actions, "and all possible questions will disappear." "And then the Crystal Palace will arise," underground man continues, "halcyon days will arrive." Life may become "dreadfully boring (for what's the point of doing anything if all is set and classified according to graphs and tables?). On the other hand, though, everything will be extremely reasonable." For underground man, something is left out of this calculus—an irreducible and insatiable desire, for a love that leads to new life "is constantly knocking all systems and theories to hell."[74]

The Crystal Palace did not merely exhibit the ability of new technologies to create a better world. It demonstrated—through displays of raw materials, machinery, and manufacturing—new divisions of labor and mechanisms for generating new sources of wealth. The Great Exhibition has been described as "a watershed moment in the development of modern-day consumer habits," and "the first outburst of the phantasmagoria of commodity culture."[75] The automation of agency presented was not ultimately concerned with human industry or potential, but rather commercial industry and profitability. This was a vision of world in which everything is predictable to be purchasable.

72. Floridi, *Fourth Revolution*, 25–28.

73. Supp-Montgomerie, *When the Medium Was the Mission*, 28.

74. Dostoevsky, *Notes from Underground*, 5, 27–29, 143.

75. Shears, *Great Exhibition*, 2.

The Industrial Revolution remade the United States into a new political and economic empire. By 1900, the agrarian nation of East Coast villages had become a nation of states and territories connecting the western and eastern coasts of North American and reaching beyond them. After destroying and displacing numerous and diverse Indigenous settlements, the US, in the words of Arthur Levine and Scott Van Pelt, had become a nation "built of steel, powered by petroleum and electricity, illuminated by gas and electric light, and crisscrossed by railroad, telegraph, and telephone lines. More than two out of every five Americans lived in cities, and a minority worked on farms." During this industrial transformation a few "industrial natives . . . born after the advent of canals, steamboats, factories, railroads, and farm technologies" consolidated technological innovations and wealth by creating financial empires: "Andrew Carnegie in steel, John D. Rockefeller in oil, Jay Gould in railroads, and J. P. Morgan in banking." The power these men had over a country "with a legal regulatory system created to govern an agrarian society" was significant, and led to price-fixing, deplorable conditions for workers, and other unjust practices.[76] Their influence over the country's institutions came through gains and goals as well as methods and models: industrial gains and goals established new universities to educate a new workforce of engineers and managers, and industrial methods and models led to standardization and scale. Education, for example, became more like a mass-production assembly line that produced credits and degrees. Efficiency increasingly became a goal as well as a means. In a 1946 foreword to *Brave New World*, which was initially published in 1932 and made Henry Ford a messianic figure of a new world order, Aldus Huxley observed, "In an age of advanced technology, inefficiency is the [unforgivable] sin against the Holy Ghost."[77]

In *The Upswing: How America Came Together a Century Ago and How We Can Do It Again*, Robert Putnam and Shaylyn Romney Garrett point to the progress realized following the social disruptions caused by the Industrial Revolution of the nineteenth century. The "utterly new world of the twentieth century—transformed by urbanization, industrialization, an increasing dependence on wage labor, the mushrooming of corporations and consolidations of every kind, the rewriting of social norms and customs, a rapidly growing and diversifying population, and raging debates

76. Levine and Van Pelt, *Great Upheaval*, 17–18, 26–27.

77. Huxley, "Foreword," in *Brave New World and Brave New World Revisited*, xxii–xxiii.

about the role of individuals, institutions, and government in managing the challenges these conditions created"—led to "a moral awakening" and "active citizenship." Reformers critiqued current economic, political, social, and cultural systems; cultivated hope and individual agency; and created "an astounding number of inventive new solutions" to address "a vast array of problems." These included free public high schools and libraries to meet the demand for more educated workers; regulations to protect workers and restrain corporations; and women's suffrage and advocacy organizations such as the NAACP for more inclusion.[78]

For more than six decades, Putnam and Garrett argue, there was "imperfect but steady . . . progress toward *greater* economic equality, *more* cooperation in the public square, a *stronger* social fabric, and a *growing* culture of solidarity." By 1960, "America had been transformed into a more egalitarian, cooperative, cohesive, and altruistic nation." It was still far from ideal, by any measure, for too much had been compromised and unrealized with regard to racial and gender rights. But the first half of the 1960s were hopeful years, and even deep criticisms of contemporary society "assumed mid-century Americans could be rallied" to their causes. Michael Harrington's *The Other America: Poverty in the United States* (1962) "helped start the Great Society"; Rachel Carson's *Silent Spring* (1962) advanced the environmental movement; James Baldwin's *The Fire Next Time* (1963) "foreshadowed the grim racial strain of the coming decades"; and Betty Friedan's *The Feminine Mystique* (1963) inspired a new feminism. "As the Sixties ended," Putnam and Garrett conclude, "so, too, it seemed, did America's promise of prosperity." And since then, "we have been experiencing *declining* economic equality, the *deterioration* of compromise in the public square, a *fraying* social fabric, and a *descent* into cultural narcissism."[79]

In 1962, Donald Knuth began working on a project that he began to publish in 1968: *The Art of Computer Programming*, called the bible of all algorithms, for which volumes are still forthcoming. With the rise of computer science in the 1960s, the third industrial revolution was well underway and the foundation for the fourth had already been laid. Second-order technologies began to be replaced with "third-order" technologies: the humanity–technology–technology relation could be replaced with technology–technology–technology structures for many activities.[80] It is not

78. Putnam and Garret, *Upswing*, 8, 317, 327, 329.

79. Putnam and Garret, *Upswing*, 10–11, 303, 310.

80. Floridi, *Fourth Revolution*, 29.

clear, however, that we as a society have grasped fully the extent to which previous industrial revolutions have challenged our attention and agency. Our technological society offers and promises more freedoms from many things—freedom from hunger, disease, ignorance, confinement, inequity, material poverty, and much more. But Albert Borgmann asks if, "underneath the surface of technological liberty and prosperity there is a sense of captivity and depression." "[W]e may hope," he adds, "that once we understand technology more incisively and clearly, there will be good news."[81]

Borgmann seems skeptical about what good may be discovered, though. He argues that the complexity of industrial technologies, along with the movement toward standardized mass production and scientific management, created "a device paradigm" that severs us from adequately understanding technology. Borgmann explains that when we see a surface good—for example, Cool Whip, an artificial whipped cream—we do not see the scientific, technological, and economic structures and processes that produce this commodity for our consumption. The result is that we have become blind to the dynamics and nature of the advanced technological culture that has emerged in industrial societies. More fundamentally, substantial things (for example, real cream) and practices (whipping the cream) have been displaced by superficial commodities and consumption.[82] Borgmann observes further that as more people began to migrate to cities, public places become spaces of observed consumption. This suggests an additional layer to Borgmann's surface–structure device paradigm—surveillance—which digital technologies exacerbate as they envelop and merge our private and public lives.

Borgmann's notions of substantial things and focal practices, displaced by the structural complexity of our industrial society, point to the importance of reflective attention, structural agency, and knowledge augmentation as significant values. For Borgmann, substantial things and focal practices are pre-industrial: he laments, for example, how televisions and microwaves have displaced reading and table fellowship. While his critique of the industrial imagination is insightful, Borgmann fails to suggest how we might imagine and create new objects and actions worthy of our attention and agency as we find ourselves in a fourth industrial revolution that is even more complex.

81. Borgmann, "Introduction," in *Power Failure*, 8.
82. Borgmann, *Power Failure*, 15–18.

A fundamental challenge we face today with information automation is the extent to which it threatens the dis-automatization connected with the origin of our species that resulted in our capacity for reflective attention. As new media emerged throughout the twentieth century, "attention merchants" found new ways to convert our attention into revenue.[83] Today, with the help of advanced techniques and tools such as AI, corporations compete for and commoditize our attention in ways that interfere with our ability to focus and do what we want to do. This functional distraction can lead to an existential form of distraction, if our higher goals and values are compromised and we are hindered from being who we want to be over time. These forms of distraction can lead to a deeper, epistemic form of distraction—a diminishment of fundamental capacities, such as reflection, imagination, reasoning, and metacognition, which enable us to define our goals and values.[84]

In addition to the threat to attention, Brett Frischmann and Evan Selinger caution about diminishing human agency. As we design new autonomous systems, they ask, are we also redesigning ourselves? "What meaningfully distinguishes *Homo sapiens* from all other species is our capability to imagine, conceptualize, and engineer ourselves and our environment," they argue, and "what matters about being human is how we exercise such power over generations to collectively produce, cultivate, and sustain shared normative conceptions of humanity." Our humanity "is reflected in us and our built world of imagined realities, institutions, infrastructures, and environments," but we need to be attentive to how our identities, societies, and world can be controlled, conditioned, and constrained by our own creations. To grapple with the impacts of twenty-first–century technologies, Frischmann and Selinger say we need to ask the following questions:

1. Who are we?

2. What sort of people do we aspire to be?

3. What values and capabilities do we possess and commit ourselves to sustain?

4. What sort of society do we want to build and sustain?

83. Wu, *Attention Merchants*, 5.

84. James Williams describes these three types of attention as "spotlight," "starlight," and "daylight." See *Stand Out of Our Light*, esp. 50, 56, 68.

5. What obligations do we owe to past, present, and the future generations? And how should such obligations shape the technological and
social institutions we build and sustain?[85]

These are important questions to keep before us, for we know that the
structural forms of autonomous agency we are capable of creating, from
cities to AI, often become oppressive and require regular human interventions to correct systemic flaws and failures.

In one of his earliest dramas, *The Rock* (1934), written for a fund-
raising campaign to build churches in the suburbs of London, T. S. Eliot
questions the health of the modern industrial society. When asked "What is
the meaning of this city?," is the answer we "huddle close together because
[we] love each other" or "We all dwell together / To make money from
each other"? "Engaged in devising the perfect refrigerator . . . in printing
as many books as possible," Eliot asks, "Where is the wisdom we have lost
in knowledge? / Where is the knowledge we have lost in information?"
Nearly one hundred years later, in a data-driven information society, we
may add, "Where is the information we have lost in data?" Reflective attention and good structural agency—the Word and work into which Eliot
calls the audience of *The Rock*—are dependent on augmenting wisdom in
"The perpetual struggle of Good and Evil."[86] While we might lament a data
deluge or information overload, Floridi points out that "complaining about
such over-abundance would be like complaining about a banquet that offers more than we can ever eat." The phenomenon of big data is a resource
to exploit, Floridi argues, "for the creation of wealth, the improvement of
human lives, and the advancement of knowledge."[87] How we may augment
knowledge and wisdom in a social and technological environment that is
increasingly hostile to truth—and can automate its negation and distractions from it—is one of the greatest challenges of our time. An appropriate
response will require systemic reforms of our information environment,
and intelligence automation can be part of the solution.

As early as the 1670s, Gottfried Leibniz articulated the possibility of
"concept-crunching machines" as well as "number crunching machines."
His ambition, Justin Smith explains, was to automate less demanding
intellectual work and "free the human mind so it may devote itself more

85. Frischmann and Selinger, *Re-Engineering Humanity*, 243, 271.
86. Eliot, *Rock*, in *Complete Poems and Plays*, 96, 98, 103–4.
87. Floridi, *Fourth Revolution*, 15–16.

fully to true and proper thinking—which is to say reflection, meditation, introspection, and the like—rather than being occupied with mere computation." Leibniz was clear that a machine could reproduce what could be called intelligent activities, such as mathematical calculation or logical inference, but this did not depend on or include machines being reflective or moral agents.[88] Understanding the actual limits and benefits of automated information processing can enable us to distinguish what intelligence automation is and how we may best use it along with human intelligence. The fourth industrial revolution has the potential to become a new knowledge revolution.

88. Smith, *Internet Is Not What You Think It Is*, 106, 119.

2

||||||||||||||||||||

Hope and Longing in Las Vegas

O ne of the most memorable trips of my childhood was to Las Vegas.
Late one summer night in 1980, the voice of my friend's father woke
me from sleep and called our attention to the colorful lights rising up from
and spreading across the horizon. The night retreated as we approached Las
Vegas, and when we entered the city there was only bright light. The following few days in the city were like being in a science fiction novel. Casinos,
the hubs of the city, were alien spaces full of electronic lights and sounds
and governed by different rules. Adults could indulge in illicit activities
nonstop, but kids had to remain off the carpets at the edges of the gambling
floors. Leaving these labyrinthine complexes, when the desert sun was so
high and hot, was so disorientating that one day I wandered into traffic and
was knocked down by a motorcycle.

When we visited Circus Circus, I had no mental model to organize
everything that was happening—the gambling activities below, the falling
and rising trapeze artists overhead, the tight ring of carnival games. My
memories are vague and certainly confused with more stable images that
came later. All I can remember clearly about the experience is that I could
not believe they let children into the place. Later, with the help of Stephen
King's *The Stand* (1978), I came to associate Las Vegas with the end of the
world. Also, in the early days of the World Wide Web, I often thought the
experience of wandering the information superhighway was like visiting
Las Vegas: information abundance and overload, casino-quality graphic
design standards, and a sense of possibility linked with luck. I was not alone
in viewing Las Vegas as an apocalyptic image of our technological society.

As our most ancient complex technology, the city—consisting of and cultivating complex technological systems, artifacts, and practices—was and remains one of the most significant innovations of our species. It is also an important image for understanding the history and future of our technological society. Las Vegas is a unique place for competing technological hopes and fears, and the surreal and strange city challenges our expectations and experiences of reality in ways that are best understood through the apocalyptic imagination. Las Vegas is an apocalyptic image of the city that can help us think about technological futures.

Welcome to Las Vegas

In the introduction to *The Unofficial Guide to Las Vegas 2019*, Bob Sehlinger observes that on a typical flight to Las Vegas travelers may be divided into two groups: those who believe they are on the way to heaven and cannot sit still in their seats, and those who are slumped in their seats convinced they are on the way to hell.[1] Las Vegas, as an adult Disneyland or Sin City, has a malleable identity—one that seems "fleeting . . . transitory, less based in anything but the human imagination."[2]

Of course every city is shaped by the human imagination, and Las Vegas is temporally grounded and physically located within a complex geographical area with its own unique natural and human histories. As an aggressively modern city, significantly shaped by technological developments such as electricity, the machine gun, nuclear weapons, and every type of entertainment and surveillance technology, Las Vegas is an important place for understanding our technological society. The real Las Vegas is, in many ways, like the cities from which its tourists come—with "subdivisions, shopping centers, boy scout troops, and churches." But the "symbolic city" of Las Vegas presents itself with an "otherworldliness" for recreation and re-creation, transforming it into a generative site for exploring fear and loathing—as well as hope and longing—related to technological innovation.[3]

Las Vegas is a city that transgresses not only regular laws, such as gambling, but typical experiences of space, time, knowledge, and agency. The

1. Sehlinger, *Unofficial Guide to Las Vegas*, 2.
2. Rothman and Davis, *Grit Beneath the Glitter*, 2.
3. Wright and Snow, "Las Vegas," 40–41.

flat, arid desert yields to fountains of water and glimmering towers. The past and the future are absorbed by an eternal present as days extend into nights filled with artificial lights. And the precarious connection between information and agency—the time or distance filled with understanding and intention—is broken through the communication of too much noise and the abduction of attention for the benefit of the house. All of this is by design.

The architectural study *Learning from Las Vegas*, published in 1972, emphasizes the hyper-artificiality of the city. Every city is an artificial environment, but the enhanced artificiality of Las Vegas does not simply control natural conditions and transcend limits through the development and use of technologies, which cities have done as long as there have been cities. Las Vegas attempts to veil natural conditions and technological limits. Viewed from without, there are massive buildings incongruous with the surrounding landscape. That bold accomplishment is as ancient as Babel. But viewed from within, spatial, temporal, epistemological, and even vocational realities are disrupted in new ways. There are big, low spaces of crowded anonymity—labyrinths that "combine being together and yet separate." These artificial enclosures, permanently enlightened oases that ignore diurnal rhythms, "expand and unify the space by obscuring its physical limits." Within these overwhelming environments, "The moving eye in the moving body must work to pick out and interpret a variety of changing, juxtaposed orders . . . 'chaos is very near.'" All of this is for recreation, which becomes re-creation as casinos "engulf the visitor in a new role."[4]

Because of the disruptive and dislocating experiences presented to visitors, which challenge our attempts to order the world, Las Vegas is perhaps best understood with an apocalyptic imagination. The luxurious city in the parched desert, which banishes the night, provides opportunities for discovery and questioning responsibilities. Viewed the right way, the city challenges and collapses the dualistic defaults with which we navigate our lives—how we separate chronological and material experiences of time and space from more meaningful or spiritual encounters, how we isolate reason from alternate sources of wisdom, and how we distinguish what is ethical or right from what a good life is and how it should be lived. Las Vegas reveals much about our real and imagined cities, our technological society, and our ultimate hopes and longings.

4. Venturi et al., *Learning from Las Vegas*, 46, 56, 58.

A Golden Age of AI

In 2011, Amazon founder Jeff Bezos pressed "his team to think bigger and to push the boundaries of established technology" to create a "device with its brain in the cloud that's completely controlled by [a] voice."[5] Amazon acquired startups for needed technologies and talent, and in late 2014 released Echo and Alexa. After the failure of Amazon's Fire Phone months earlier, Echo and Alexa were introduced with a modest press release and a two-minute explanatory YouTube video—not as a fully conversational computer, but as a device capable of performing some discrete tasks.[6] The launch was successful, stimulating rapid adoption and development, and Amazon was on its way to becoming one of the most significant leaders of AI innovation in the world.[7]

Amazon held its first public AI visioning event in Las Vegas in 2019, and the apocalyptic city of Las Vegas provided an ideal landscape for reflecting on the impact of AI on our society. In an announcement for this event on machine learning, automation, robotics, and space—called "re:MARS"—Bezos claimed, "We're at the beginning of a golden age of AI. Recent advancements have already led to invention that previously lived in the realm of science fiction—and we've only scratched the surface of what's possible." "We're excited to create re:MARS," he added, "to share learnings and spark new ideas for future innovation." Like its invitation-only predecessor MARS, begun a few years earlier, the open-to-the-public re:MARS conference embraced "an optimistic vision for scientific discovery to advance a golden age of innovation." By sharing and exploring innovations in machine learning, automation, robotics, and space exploration, Bezos hoped that re:MARS would inspire and initiate developments in AI to shape the future.[8]

With re:MARS, Amazon presented itself to the public as a company thoroughly focused on and driven by the potential of AI. It also positioned itself as a collaborative business partner and social catalyst for shaping a future enabled by AI. In the opening keynote, senior Amazon executive Dave Limp celebrated the "incredibly diverse group of people" that was in

5. Stone, *Amazon Unbound*, 24. Later in 2011, Apple released Siri on the iPhone 4S.

6. See Stone, *Amazon Unbound*, 45.

7. Bezos was enthusiastic about computer vision as well as computer voice recognition, but the contemporaneous experiment that resulted in Amazon Go took much longer to realize. See Stone, *Amazon Unbound*, 55, 68.

8. Amazon, "We're at the Beginning of a Golden Age of AI."

attendance: "Astronauts, CEOs, artists, engineers, PhDs, politicians, and of course business leaders of all types"—thousands of people from around the world. Speaking to the purpose of what was hoped to be an inaugural event, Limp described the library in one of Bezos's homes:

> There are two fireplaces that face each other. On one side of the library, over the fireplace, he has the word Builders, and under that is all of the books in his collection that are authored by builders. And on the other side of the library, it says Dreamers and he has books by Dreamers. This is a very good representation of what we are trying to do here—to bring together the builders and the dreamers—as we envision the future.

The gap is narrowing between builders and dreamers, Limp claimed. If we can imagine it, we can build it—and solve today's most interesting challenges with AI.[9] In the next keynote, senior executive Jeff Wilke cast an even more ambitious vision: "We are only in the beginning stages of truly understanding the potential for [AI] to change our lives and to help us work on some of the most important and urgent problems that humanity faces." "I believe [AI] will continue to transform our lives for the better," he confessed. AI is "one of the most powerful . . . tools humans have ever created. It holds the promise of conquering the most daunting challenges, like exploring space or curing cancer." Corporations, Wilke added, "can and should be pioneers . . . their discoveries should in turn benefit society at large."[10]

In addition to keynotes from Amazon executives, the re:MARS program included informational sessions and hands-on workshops, technology demonstrations, social events with gambling, race cars, battle bots, and a culminating fireside chat with Bezos. During that chat, Bezos was asked about the inscriptions over his library fireplaces. Bezos commented on how human creativity needs both dreamers and builders: "The dreamers come and the builders get inspired by them. And the builders build a new foundation that the dreamers can stand on and dream more." Bezos pointed out that Alexa, named after the Library of Alexandria, was inspired by the *Star Trek* computer. He also talked about the importance of taking risks and making big business bets.[11]

---

9. "Amazon re:MARS."
10. "Amazon re:MARS."
11. Bort, "Jeff Bezos Explains."

The AI technologies showcased at re:MARS 2019—recommendation systems for purchases, prediction systems for the fulfillment and delivery of purchases, robots sorting and moving packages in warehouses, and everything that enables Alexa to respond to and anticipate customer inquiries—are impressive systems that accomplish a variety of specific goals. This is narrow or soft AI, not general or strong AI. As Bezos admits, "We're still a long way from being able to have machines do things the way humans do things."[12] The many manifestations of human creativity exhibited at re:MARS, from autonomous drones to smart prosthetics, revealed that, in the words of Amazon's Chief Technology Officer Werner Vogels, "AI is enabling a new way of life." One Amazon employee in attendance said of the event: "It makes you dream for the future and just gets you so excited to see where the world is going."[13]

Because of its massive wealth, power, scale, and impact, before the COVID-19 pandemic Amazon was being criticized for its asymmetrical influence over markets, employees, and customers—and these criticisms intensified during the pandemic. Due to the pandemic, the second re:MARS conference scheduled for June 2020 in Las Vegas was canceled, and dreams about AI solving future business and social challenges were largely displaced by a global health crisis. For Amazon, this meant managing unprecedented demand for online purchasing, scaling up physical infrastructure to fulfill that demand, and nearly doubling its human workforce to do what could not be done with machine learning, automation, and robots. Bezos, who preferred to spend his time on big bets "whose potential was years in the future . . . locked his gaze firmly onto the urgent present" and became closely involved in the daily operations of what had already become "one of the largest and most sophisticated logistics and transportation networks anywhere."[14]

Like many organizations, Amazon attempted to find technological solutions—especially with AI—to respond to the pandemic. On April 1, the Stanford Institute for Human-Centered Artificial Intelligence (HAI) hosted a virtual conference on COVID-19 and AI.[15] A number of promising efforts were presented based on the usefulness of AI for "finding patterns across

12. Bezos, *Invent and Wonder*, 213.

13. "Amazon re:MARS."

14. Stone, *Amazon Unbound*, 213, 387.

15. See https://hai.stanford.edu/events/covid-19-and-ai-virtual-conference.

multiple data types."[16] These efforts included using AI to process medical literature for relevant findings, X-ray images for diagnosing patients, patient electronic health records for risks, geolocation data for monitoring infections, and genomic data for creating vaccines. A few months later, HAI hosted a much more sober virtual conference titled "COVID + AI: The Road Ahead."[17] This conference focused less on AI and more on the economic and political crises that were exacerbating the health and social impacts of the pandemic. HAI's spring 2021 conference, also virtual, was titled "Intelligence Augmentation: AI Empowering People to Solve Global Challenges" and did not focus on COVID-19.[18]

The trajectory of those three HAI conferences reflects the pattern of much social-technological discourse associated with the pandemic. Hopes were tested, frustrated, and recast. Initially, there were great hopes for technological solutions: surely recent advances in AI would enable us to understand and respond to COVID-19. There certainly were significant technological solutions: the sharing of open data and code via the internet, the rapid production of vaccines, and the scalable digital technologies that enabled many activities to continue online are all well-known successes. The latest AI advances, however, do not seem to have been the most important pandemic technologies. Indeed, AI may be remembered as one of the most abused technologies during the pandemic as an amplifier of false information. As for Amazon, its successes in AI did not include its systems for "mass-managing people." From hiring through firing, Amazon's "maze of systems that maximized efficiency and minimized human contact" was "uneven and strained" before the pandemic. According to a June 15, 2021 *New York Times* exposé, these systems "burned through workers, resulted in inadvertent firings and stalled benefits, and impeded communication."[19] On July 1, 2021, Amazon announced two new leadership principles, which are meant to guide day-to-day operations: "Strive to be Earth's Best Employer," and "Success and Scale Bring Broad Responsibility."[20]

Amazon set a new earnings record in 2020 and Bezos, confident about Amazon's future, stepped down from his role of CEO to pursue other bets.

16. Pena, "Stanford Virtual Conference."

17. See https://hai.stanford.edu/events/covid-ai-road-ahead.

18. See https://hai.stanford.edu/events/2021-spring-conference-intelligence-augmentation-ai-empowering-people-solve-global.

19. Kantor et al., "Inside Amazon's Employment Machine."

20. Soper, "Amazon Adds Two New Leadership Principles."

The day after he flew into space in one of his Blue Origin rockets, the 2021 Alexa Live *virtual* developer's conference highlighted the increased use and accelerated development of Alexa during the pandemic—especially in homes, the automation of which is one of Amazon's next big bets. Presenting from Amazon's Spheres in downtown Seattle, significantly emptied by the pandemic, executives shared their vision for making AI assistants a natural part of our lives—always present and listening, always learning and adapting, and always becoming more personal and proactive.[21]

Initial hopes for AI may have been checked by the pandemic, but instead of sober assessments about the real impacts of AI during the pandemic, new post-pandemic hopes emerged. As we engage with the digital dimension of the factories of our new industrial era that extend into our homes and workplaces—places merging or linked through digitally enabled labor—AI is guiding the organization of machine cities such as Amazon's warehouses. These systems are also transforming our homes and cities into Edens optimized by and for AI models, and we are right to wonder where humans fit within and/or outside these automated loops of inputs and outputs. Amazon and other companies that have gambled on the potential and promises of AI have realized a number of business successes, but what will winning and losing look like in our AI society? Two critics of the technological city—both working nearer the dawn of AI, and both inspired by the Apocalypse—can help us reflect on our current structural gambles: Jacques Ellul and Hunter S. Thompson.

A Rejection of the City

In 1970, Ellul published in English what is perhaps his most important theological work, *The Meaning of the City*. A French version appeared in 1975. Ellul had been working on the text since the late 1940s, following his participation in the French Resistance against Nazi Germany and the Vichy regime. At the same time, his most sustained and definitive sociological analysis of modern technological civilization was taking shape. This was published in French in 1954, with the title *Technique or the Wager of the Century* (*La Technique ou l'enjeu du siècle*), and in English in 1964, with the simpler title *The Technological Society*. Ellul explained the two books were composed in "counterpoint": "To my book on technology corresponds my

21. See https://developer.amazon.com/en-US/alexa/alexa-live.

theologically based study of the great city as the supreme achievement" of human technology. It has become common, therefore, to read *The Meaning of the City* as Ellul's theological interpretation of *The Technological Society*.[22]

In *The Technological Society*, Ellul focuses on much more than modern technologies. By "technique" he means "the totality of methods rationally arrived at and having absolute efficiency . . . in every field of human activity."[23] He describes how humanity made a wager "on technology in the twentieth century"—i.e., on rationalized efficiency characteristic of technological methodology—and concludes, "Technology had won the bet and proceeded to beat the house."[24] Like a physician in the midst of an epidemic, Ellul offers a diagnosis of the disease rather than suggesting a cure. And his diagnosis is bleak. The modern technological society has evolved into an autonomous force or agency, which creates its own "artificial necessity." Technology now "pursues its own course more and more independently" of humans. He explains:

> This means that man participates less and less actively in technical creation, which, by the automatic combination of prior elements, becomes a kind of fate. Man is reduced to the level of a catalyst. Better still, he resembles a slug [or token] inserted into a slot machine: he starts the operation without participating in it.[25]

In a nearly fatalistic conclusion, Ellul claims: "It is vanity to pretend [technique] can be checked or guided . . . the human race is beginning confusedly to understand at last that it is living in a new and unfamiliar universe." "Enclosed within [our] artificial creation," he concludes, we find that there is "no exit"—we cannot pierce the shell of our monolithic technological culture. And yet, Ellul cautions, technological determinism is a false necessity. The response is not about "getting rid of [technology], but, by an act of freedom, transcending it." Given the monolithic power of the technological phenomenon, Ellul suggests three "possible disturbing phenomena" or potential disruptions: war, collective revolt, and divine intervention. But in the end, he appeals to individual responsibility and resistance: for "each one of us" to not abdicate "responsibilities with regard to values," and to not limit ourselves "to leading a trivial existence in a technological civilization, with greater adaptation and increasing success" as

22. Prior, *Confronting Technology*, 164.

23. Ellul, *Technological Society*, xxv.

24. Russo, *Future Without a Past*, 12.

25. Ellul, *Technological Society*, 135.

our sole objective. He warns: "If we do not even consider the possibility of making a stand against these determinants, then . . . the determinants *will* be transformed into inevitabilities."[26]

In his exegesis of the biblical image of the city in *The Meaning of the City*, Ellul sees divine intervention as the necessary "disturbing phenomenon." For the meaning of the city is that it is a curse that only God can correct. Ellul reads the story of Cain establishing the first city as an act of rebellion against God and a "failure to recognize God's work."[27] As a "counter-creation" that "breaks with the divine nature of creation," the city represents humans' rejection of truth for a false reality, autonomy, and intelligence. But in creating the city, humanity's greatest technological accomplishment, humans create "something stronger than [themselves]," "an autonomous power." A city becomes an artificial, autonomous, adversarial, and multi-agent system with its own objectives: control, certainty, closure, and commodification. The diabolical human city, Ellul concludes, "cannot be reformed" or redeemed. It stands condemned and must be "replaced" and re-created by God at the "end of time, but absolutely not by any human effort."[28]

In the end, God "adopts" and "takes charge" of what humans have manufactured—outside of and even against God's creation and intentions. God "becomes a builder."[29] New Jerusalem, which comes down from heaven at the end of the Apocalypse, is built by God alone, Ellul claims. This is something of an affirmation of human creativity, but Ellul sees in God's final or eschatological acts a rejection of human artifacts and artificial agency: only humans, not their powerful technologies, may participate in new creation.[30] Ellul focuses on the agency of Jesus Christ, in whom "all things" in heaven and on earth are united. This potentially includes both "technical failures" and "the marvels of [human] cleverness," but Ellul concludes we do not know what will be preserved. We are promised God's

---

26. Ellul, *Technological Society*, xxix–xxx, xxxiii, 428–29.

27. An alternative reading would see Cain's city, an artificial creation named after the natural creation of the son he named Enoch, as more of a blessing. Through the city and descendants of Enoch come the blessings of the arts and sciences.

28. Ellul, *Meaning of the City*, 35, 50, 52, 54, 57, 59, 63, 70, 77, 109, 154, 163.

29. Ellul, *Meaning of the City*, 102–3, 176.

30. See Prior, *Confronting Technology*, 77–79.

city, "but with no explanatory details, of all that made up the glory of the nations"—i.e., what humans may bring into the city.[31]

Until the end, technology and the technological society are thoroughly captive to powers and principalities greater than us. Humans and our works are "radically evil"; we live in the condemned city and not in "contact" with New Jerusalem. Although we know that in the end the city will be pardoned, "this is a revelation of God's grace and is absolutely not to be forced into the present course of things." "Realizing that the new Jerusalem is not a work of our hands," Ellul concludes, "the whole affair will boil down to our rejection by the city."[32] Humans are active participants in history, but this role has more to do with being a witness of God's city and of God's judgment against the human city. In his book on the Apocalypse of John, Ellul asserts, "Hope, as we see it in the Apocalypse, implies the total rejection of the confusion between the Kingdom of God and any kind of politico-social system" or human civilization. The judgement of Babylon is a "*double* condemnation" of every state and "all cities, those of the past and those of the present." In Ellul's reading of the Apocalypse, "New creation, which is absolutely new, comes only through judgment and destruction . . . There is no continuity." Babylon, not the City of God, is the end of human progress. New Jerusalem is God's reversal of "what had been the instrument of revolt . . . to make of it the work of reconciliation."[33]

Ellul would have—and indeed may have—seen Las Vegas as a confirmation of his notions about the doomed destiny of the technological city and society. And he would not be alone. Richard Mouw writes in *Calvinism in the Las Vegas Airport*, that Las Vegas

> seems to be despised by thinkers across the theological spectrum. Christian conservatives hate Las Vegas because of its gambling, booze, and promiscuity; liberals because of its greed, bad taste, and sexism.

And yet, Mouw observes, "Some of the things people mention when they talk about Las Vega are also things the Bible says about the 'new Jerusalem' . . . People go to Las Vegas with deep yearning for security and satisfaction. It is a place that symbolizes promise. Its psychic currency is the stuff of which our dreams are made." Las Vegas may be a "counterfeit version of the

31. Ellul, *Meaning of the City*, 176.

32. Ellul, *Meaning of the City*, 176, 178–79, 182.

33. Ellul, *Apocalypse*, 26, 59, 196–97, 214–15, 223.

'new Jerusalem,'" but "it shares something of the glorious reality it mocks
... It calls to us, but it does not deliver on its promises."[34]

A Judgment of the City

As Ellul was working on his parallel projects of critiquing the technological society and condemning the technological city, Hunter S. Thompson
was working on a variety of journalistic and fictional projects exploring his
sense of vocation as well as his view of his country. These explorations became more focused as his fears of the 1960s eclipsed his hopes for that decade. The assassination of John F. Kennedy, in particular, filled Thompson
with fear about the future of America and loathing for ideologues on both
sides of the political spectrum competing to shape it.[35] What this meant
for him—a "maverick with an outlaw bent searching for the unvarnished
truth in a fast-paced, irrational Cold-War World"[36]—was finding a style
that powerfully expressed his sense of rightness.[37] This style, which blended
journalism, fiction, and autobiography, became the "total subjectivity" of
Gonzo journalism.[38]

In 1966, Thompson left California and settled into his rural retreat in
Woody Creek, Colorado, outside of Aspen. He declared California, where
he had witnessed a countercultural "revolution of expectations," to be a
nightmare of failed possibilities. He believed the revolution had failed, and
he signed a contract to write a polemic on the topic of "The Death of the
American Dream."[39] This project presented Thompson with a number of
questions. What was the American Dream? What were the ideals that in
Abraham Lincoln's words, which Thompson often quoted, made the US

34. Mouw, *Calvinism in the Las Vegas Airport*, 94–95, 101.

35. Thompson seems to have first used the phrase "fear and loathing" in a letter written after the Kennedy assassination. Two years later, he wrote that Lee Harvey Oswald
"wrote the ending" to the great American novel. Thompson, *Proud Highway*, 420, 530.

36. Brinkley, "Editor's Note," xxii.

37. In a letter to his mother in 1957, referencing the book *The Outsider*, Thompson
said the outlaw isn't wrong—he just doesn't "express his rightness correctly." Thompson,
Proud Highway, 67. Thompson defined an outlaw "as somebody who lives outside the
law, beyond the law, not necessarily against it." Thompson, quoted in Nuttall, "Apocalypse and Hell," 112.

38. Streitfeld, ed., *Hunter S. Thompson*, 35.

39. McKeen, *Outlaw Journalist*, 114.

"the last, best hope" of humanity?[40] If the "Dream" was about freedom and possibility, had these great hopes been lost—and, if so, how? Could they be realized still? In 1971, Thompson retreated to Las Vegas to interview the activist attorney Oscar Zeta Acosta, where they could be free from police surveillance. He funded the trip by accepting a *Sports Illustrated* assignment to cover the Mint 400 desert off-road race. While there, the city inspired him to begin writing about his hopes and fears. Thompson returned a month later with another assignment, from *Rolling Stone*, to cover a narcotics convention, and he resumed his search for the American Dream.

The resulting book, *Fear and Loathing in Las Vegas: A Savage Journey to the Heart of the American Dream*, is divided into two parts, one for each of the assignments that funded Thompson's trips to the city. There are two abused convertibles, two trashed hotel rooms, and a series of drug-fueled episodes surrounding the two events on which he was supposed to report. These were not uninteresting topics to him (motorcycles and drugs), but his real "very ominous assignment" was "to find the American Dream." This story would not be "a classic affirmation of everything right and true and decent in the national character . . . [a] salute to the fantastic *possibilities* of life in this country." The story he sought, "the main story of [his] generation," was about loss, about "some other era, burned out and long gone from the brutish realities of [the] foul year of Our Lord, 1971."[41] Thompson himself described the book as "the definitive epitaph statement for the Benevolent Drug Era of the 60s," which he expected would be followed by a "far more vicious time" of fear and loathing.[42]

Each part of the book ends with a lament. At the end of the first part, Thompson laments the loss of a sense of hope and promise he had experienced in San Francisco:

> There was a fantastic universal sense that whatever we were doing was *right*, that we were winning. . . . that sense of inevitable victory over the forces of Old and Evil. Not in any mean or military sense; we didn't need that. Our energy would simply *prevail*. There was no sense in fighting—on our side or theirs. We had all the momentum; we were riding the crest of a high and beautiful wave . . . So now, less than five years later, you can go up on steep hill in Las Vegas and look West, and with the right kind of eyes you can

40. Brinkley, "Editor's Note," xxvii.
41. Thompson, *Fear and Loathing in Las Vegas*, 6, 18, 19, 23.
42. Thompson, *Fear and Loathing in America*, 428.

almost *see* the high-water mark—that place where the wave finally broke and rolled back.

Before this lament, and before the lament that comes at the end of the second part of the book, Thompson writes about Circus Circus, which functions as a synecdoche for Las Vegas. With its nonstop gambling, wild circus acts, and loud carnival activities, the place was an affront to reality when "Reality itself is too twisted." Thompson twice calls it the "main nerve" of the debased American Dream. And what is the new form of this dream? The myth of winning when the house is against you—"that vision of the Big Winner somehow emerging from the last-minute pre-dawn chaos of a stale Vegas casino." This myth is kept alive by stories such as the Circus Circus owner's: "he always wanted to run away and join the circus when he was a kid . . . Now the bastard has his own circus, and a license to steal, too."[43]

For Thompson, Las Vegas reflected a new dark age in America, where dreams of freedom and possibility had been reduced to desperate narcissistic and nihilistic pursuits. Here, he writes, "the shark ethic prevails—eat the wounded. In a closed society where everybody's guilty, the only crime is getting caught. In a world of thieves, the only final sin is stupidity." In the book's final lament, Thompson concludes, "We are all wired into a *survival trip* now." Drugs for engagement (uppers) and ideas about "consciousness expansion" had been replaced with drugs for escape (downers) and a loss of faith in "that Light at the end of the tunnel."[44] In the final chapter, Thompson himself turns to "drugs that shrink perception to pusillanimous narcissism . . . to sedate himself."[45] And he makes himself into an incarnation of the American Nightmare.[46]

In the "postwar garden" of Las Vegas, at the edge of American expansion, Thompson saw how human freedom and potential could be deformed in an avaricious, automated, and artificial reality.[47] This was the dawn of the commercial information age, and Thompson witnessed a "loveless monetarism, a robotic emptiness in the clattering of dice or the clicking of the roulette wheel where algorithms bloom in the desert." There were automatic luxury cars, hidden computers financially sorting people and

43. Thompson, *Fear and Loathing in Las Vegas*, 47–48, 57, 68, 191.

44. Thompson, *Fear and Loathing in Las Vegas*, 72, 178–79.

45. McEneaney, *Hunter S. Thompson*, 159.

46. This "overshadowing persona" came to eclipse his status as a "serious thinker and writer." McKeen, "Two Sides of Hunter S. Thompson," 8.

47. Rothman and Davis, *Grit Beneath the Glitter*, 2.

optimizing operations, impersonalized services, and robot-like people serving extractive mechanisms for predictable and controllable outcomes. Hope and even the "possibility" of love [had been reduced] to narcissistic fantasy."[48] Playing with high-tech vehicles, communication devices, pharmaceuticals, and weapons, Thompson was not interested in rejecting technology. But he raged against a technological society that suppressed freedom and possibility through mercenary systems, merciless laws, and restrictive state and private surveillance. For Thompson, Las Vegas was a manifestation of the technological city and society without a moral foundation. The "Dream"—American or any other—"can only exist within a moral landscape." In Thompson's America, this morality "had gone AWOL."[49]

In *Fear and Loathing in Las Vegas*, Thompson abandoned the American realist tradition for a style that "indicates apocalyptic affinities" with more imaginative literary traditions. Gonzo, variously defined, is essentially about transforming reality through an imaginative enhancement of it. It

> goes against the limits, turns the ordinary into perpetual carnival, a maelstrom of living on the edge and tipping over into an Other-world of transcendence where anything remains possible, including decoding the savage heart of the American Dream in a casino or hotel room in Las Vegas.[50]

This is writing that can "remake, rewrite, and reimagine," and one could describe it as a product of the apocalyptic imagination.[51] The book of Revelation was one of Thompson's "favorite pieces of writing,"[52] and a "key source" for his "apocalyptically wild" work.[53] The Apocalypse was one of the few things he read about which he said, "Boy, I wish I could write that," and he claimed he would read it when he needed to "get cranked up about language" that would not be merely informative but provocative.[54] Thompson plundered the Apocalypse for captivating poetic imagery, admitting that he had "stolen more quotes and thoughts and purely elegant little starbursts of writing from the Book of Revelation than anything else in the English

---

48. McEneaney, *Hunter S. Thompson*, 113.

49. Nuttall, "Apocalypse and Hell," 105.

50. McEneaney, *Hunter S. Thompson*, 113, 163.

51. Alexander and Isager, *Fear and Loathing Worldwide*, 5.

52. McKeen, *Outlaw Journalist*, 215.

53. Alexander and Isager, *Fear and Loathing Worldwide*, 3–4.

54. Thompson, *Ancient Gonzo Wisdom*, 205, 235.

language." He loved "the wild power of the language and the purity of the madness that governs it and makes it music."[55]

The imaginative power of the Apocalypse helped Thompson interpret Las Vegas as a metaphor for the depraved state of the American Dream, and perhaps even discover signs of hope. As Douglas Brinkley observes, *Fear and Loathing in Las Vegas* is a "scathing denunciation of American culture, yet at the same time it's a celebration of American culture."[56] In other words, fear and loathing had not completely displaced hope and longing in Thompson's judgment of the city. Perhaps this explains why Thompson wrote two additional endings for the book, acknowledging that the published version was not a proper ending.[57] After his second lament, he writes: "no solace for refugees, no point in looking back. The question, as always, is *now* . . . ?"[58] The question of whether or not humans may "achieve the freedom and love they imagine to be possible" is literally left open with a question mark.[59] As his political activism before and after *Fear and Loathing in Las Vegas* reveals, Thompson very much desired and worked for a new *polis* in spite of his judgment of the present one.[60] His method involved subversive interventions—refusing to function as a slug in the machine—introducing creative chaos in an attempt to stall the system.[61]

55. McKeen, *Outlaw Journalist*, 312.

56. Quoted in McKeen, *Outlaw Journalist*, 169.

57. See McEneaney, *Hunter S. Thompson*, 160.

58. Thompson, *Fear and Loathing in Las Vegas*, 180.

59. McEneaney, *Hunter S. Thompson*, 171.

60. In 1970, Thompson ran for county sheriff. His next book after *Fear and Loathing in Las Vegas* was *Fear and Loathing: On the Campaign Trail '72*, covering the Nixon–McGovern presidential race.

61. Thompson uses drugs in *Fear and Loathing* as a vehicle for revelation: "The drugs offer sublime revelations about unveiling the depraved depths of the nightmare . . . if you can open your eyes and see reality for what it is beneath the hypocritical mask." But *Fear and Loathing* also can be read as a critique of drug culture, "revealing and exposing how drugs were about to ruin the American Dream through futile police enforcement that would criminalize many innocents, and through cultural self-destruction whereby the best minds of his generation would be destroyed, not merely by conformity . . . but through overindulgence in a pharmaceutical explosion that would lead to debilitating addiction for a large percentage of the nation's population." Thompson admitted in *Fear and Loathing* that drugs were "almost irrelevant" in Vegas (190), and Thompson's editor at Random House wrote that "it was 'absolutely clear' to him that neither Thompson nor Acosta were on drugs in the novel." McEneaney, *Hunter S. Thompson*, 87, 113–14, 172.

Learning from Las Vegas

When I returned to Las Vegas in 1995, casinos on the strip had morphed into family-friendly gambling theme parks with "world-class spectacles and illusions."[62] Since then, the corporate ordering of the city through consolidation and standardization has transformed much of the original chaos of the city into a predictable entertainment experience like Disneyland. The city seems "systematically planned, highly polished, absolutely regimented, and totally plastic."[63] AI is everywhere. The hospitality industry "has been very aggressive about adopting new technologies," such as virtual concierge programs, slot machines with facial recognition for personalized services, crowd-tracking technology to optimize casino floor layouts, and other proactive "behind-the-scenes" applications that casinos will not disclose.[64] (An interesting application of gaming and hospitality AI is the University of Nevada at Las Vegas's virtual president, a "personable chat bot that can help connect students with resources and check in on their health and well-being."[65]) The old renegade Vegas Thompson ripped through in 1971 may have been transformed into a new corporate Vegas, but the city still reflects, as David Wright and Robert Snow observed in 1979, "a sense of uncertainty about the responsible and fulfilling paths through the technological landscape."[66]

After the high-energy keynotes at re:MARS 2019, business leaders, developers, and others presented projects and plans for enhancing our lives with AI. These were often interesting and inspiring, but ambitions seemed both technologically complex and modest. AI may create many previously unimagined and delightful consumer experiences, but one needs to spend some time lounging in casino bars to find those who—unconcerned with flawed datasets and opaque models—are speaking about world-saving or world-ending forms of imagined AI. What has been accomplished with AI to date is impressive, but the role of AI during the pandemic challenged hype and hopes. AI technologies facilitated the spread of misinformation and disinformation about the pandemic and vaccines, and some of these technologies were used in surveillance systems

---

62. Rothman and Davis, *Grit Beneath the Glitter*, 2.
63. Sehlinger, *Unofficial Guide to Las Vegas*, 4.
64. Shoro, "Artificial Intelligence Making More Inroads into Las Vegas Casinos."
65. Whitford, "UNLV President Turns Himself Into an AI."
66. Wright and Snow, "Las Vegas," 61.

with negative impacts in workplaces, online classrooms, and in public spaces.

People living in 1970 could, if they desired, understand most of the technologies they used. They may have noticed, as Ellul and Thompson did, that technical mechanisms and social systems were becoming more complex and manipulative, but the consumer products they used—telephones, typewriters, audio-visual equipment—were understandable. Today, all of these operations may be performed on a mobile phone, a device that functions in ways that are technologically and economically opaque to most of us. Technological complexity is an integral part of our lives now. As Shadbolt and Hampson note, "No individual modern human could make a smartphone."[67] And few truly understand the dynamics of the complex systems to which it connects us.

Clearly, we are still learning how AI technologies may be used and abused. Not far from the casinos in downtown Las Vegas and on the strip, at the Mob Museum and the National Atomic Testing Museum (respectively), visitors to the city can explore two of the most important technological legacies from the twentieth century: the machine gun and the atomic bomb. The machine gun was created with a single purpose: to kill more people more efficiently. Nuclear energy technologies, however, have multiple uses, from civilian power plants to military weapons (although currently we are most concerned with nuclear weapons waiting to be used for their designed ends). These technologies should not only remind us of the Babylonian dangers that can taint our greatest ambitions, but of the need to reform old and form new structures of shared agency—and, most importantly, maintain artificers' agency over artifactual agency.

Ellul and Thompson point out important challenges of structural agency in our technological society. Ellul provides a helpful diagnosis of the asymmetrical powers of autonomous systems, which have only increased with advances in AI. But Ellul could not imagine a viable disruption of such systems, and he saw little hope for the human city and the technological society. In his view, human aspirations cannot go beyond the constraints of predictable expectations—the logic of artificial systems overwhelms and prevails. Thompson's critical distance from autonomous systems helped reveal their merciless operations, but his acts of rebellion introduced minor disruptions and did not satisfy his desire for a better country. For Thompson, hope devolved into fear and longing became loathing.

67. Shadbolt and Hampson, *Digital Ape*, 43.

While the Apocalypse helped both Ellul and Thompson critique the technological society, both viewed it negatively as a condemnation of human depravity and creativity. For Ellul, Christ would redeem human creativity eschatologically at the end of time. Thompson, unable to reject human creativity both deformed and transformed by the city and the technological society, looked elsewhere for hope and transformation. In their readings of the Apocalypse, both missed not only the fullness of the divine affirmation of the city but also how that affirmation transforms every human city into a medium of new creation. In the Apocalypse, a greater agency—divine and human—not only disrupts but transforms autonomous systems, and ultimate hopes and longings are realized in and through the technological city.

On the fiftieth anniversary of *Fear and Loathing in Las Vegas*, one Las Vegas writer described Thompson as "a tourist on a mission." The resident knows "Las Vegas as two cities. One is ours and one is theirs . . . their idea of what the city means or represents is necessarily very different from the one those of us who live here experience." Another Las Vegas writer noted: "The fiction is that Vegas is a shallow, hollow place and the Strip is the worst example of depravity and consumerism. In actuality, Vegas is an inspiring city . . . Love for Las Vegas can only be conjured by the reality of the place itself."[68] Like every city, Las Vegas is both an image of the city and the reality of the city. It is also, like every city, host to deformative and transformative dimensions of our technological society. In the Apocalypse, these two dimensions are named Babylon and New Jerusalem and humans participate in both. One of these cities is doomed to fall with evil technologies; the other is destined to triumph with good technologies.

---

68. Diamond et al., "How Las Vegas Locals Really Feel about 'Fear and Loathing.'"

3

||||||||||||||||||||

The Apocalypse

From the beginning, cities have both solved and created problems. In history and imagination the status of the city is often ambiguous—it is a technological site of ingenuity but also iniquity, of innovation and injustice, of prosperity and inequity, of inspiration and desperation. As we consider the impact of new complex technologies associated with our current information revolution, including automated and autonomous technologies, the Apocalypse of John—especially its vision of the final or ultimate city—is worthy of attention.

The Apocalypse is a book for and about cities, and the city is its governing image. Like other apocalyptic texts, the Apocalypse functions to open up readers' and hearers' imaginations to perceive heaven meeting earth, the future in the present, and humans as divinely called transformative agents. All of this is revealed within a narrative about a new and better world being established by a sovereignty greater than the apparent rulers of the world. Cities are central in and for this narrative, as places of radical hope and action. The Apocalypse, a circular letter addressed to seven first-century assemblies or churches in Roman Asia Minor, addresses present conditions in each church and city. Letters to the churches are supplemented with apocalyptic images uncovering and revealing what God has done, is doing, and will do. The narrative of the Apocalypse reaches its climax with the destruction of the last evil city, Babylon, and ends with the establishment of the lasting good city of God, New Jerusalem. Although initially written for ancient cities, the Apocalypse concerns the destiny of every city—and how a new reality is situated in and being realized through them. The city is revealed as the locus and *telos* of God's new creation.

Recovering the Apocalyptic Imagination

Scholars today recognize that the apocalyptic imagination had a formative role in early Christianity. But because the Apocalypse and other apocalyptic texts have been used to fuel "fanatical millenarian expectation" or end-of-the-world enthusiasts, this theological resource is often left to its abusers. Recent efforts to overcome the theological reluctance with or prejudice against the apocalyptic imagination have focused on its historical development within ancient Jewish prophecy.[1] According to Anathea Portier-Young, the Jewish apocalyptic imagination took shape within imperial contexts, especially Hellenistic and Roman, and cultivated strategies of resistance. Apocalypses such as Daniel functioned to orient "a terrorized people through [historical] traumas to a vision of a future ordered by divine justice." Prophetic apocalyptic visions of the past, present, and future "asserted the transience and finitude of temporal powers," "articulated a resistant counterdiscourse to the discourse of empire," and "environed, advocated, and empowered resistant action."[2]

In *History and Eschatology*, N. T. Wright argues that modern philosophy—the Enlightenment, broadly understood—separates divine from human knowledge, heaven from earth, and eternity from time. Human knowledge, the earth, and the present are so radically separate from divine knowledge, heaven, and the future that these "supernatural" things can be dismissed as irrelevant or escapist. This separation results in a dualistic approach to discussions about human identity, agency, and futures. The perceived gulf between God and the world results in secular optimism in some autonomous agency, whether that is natural selection or technological progress, or in spiritual escapism, such as souls escaping to heaven.

When considering the life of Jesus, Wright argues this modern worldview fails to understand the Jewish worldview that shaped Jesus and his world. This worldview included a non-dualistic view of eschatology, which saw heaven meeting earth in the temple, the future present in the Sabbath, and humans as divine agents. In apocalyptic prophecy—which heightened

1. Collins, *Apocalyptic Imagination*, 1.
2. Portier-Young, *Apocalypse against Empire*, 50, 383.

the contrasts between human and divine knowledge, space, time, and agency—the goal was to uncover and reveal the integrated and interlocking nature of these seemingly disparate dimensions of reality. In Jewish apocalyptic literature, the transformation of the present world came with "the end of the present state of affairs." But the expectation "was for a great transformation, not for the end of the world." "Apocalyptic," Wright claims, "is about a major upheaval *within* the space-time world. We have no evidence of people thinking the world itself would end."[3]

Recovering a non-dualistic Jewish eschatology and understanding of the apocalyptic imagination enables us to see more clearly the modifications early Christians made to that worldview. "The earliest church's testimony to Jesus' resurrection precipitated a radical mutation within Jewish understanding of history and eschatology," Wright says, and reframed apocalyptic expectations: "Jesus' rising was interpreted simultaneously as a very strange event within the present world *and* the foundational and paradigmatic event within God's *new* creation." The early Christians claimed that the hoped-for transformation had "already been inaugurated through the death of Jesus and his resurrection." The Christian apocalyptic imagination, with a significantly realized eschatology, thus "opens up a vision of new creation which precisely overlaps with, and radically transforms, the present creation." Apprehending "the *real* world in its new mode," Christians claimed that in Jesus "we see revealed the true Image of God . . . revealing the new way of being human."[4]

Technological apocalypses, such as Čapek's *R.U.R.* and its successors, are often informed by a limited apocalyptic imagination. These narratives are largely negative, shaped by end-of-the-world fears rather than hopes for a better world. They also often assume a dualism that separates the secular from the sacred, leaving the latter to be ignored or left over as a place of escape. Moreover, even if our technological apocalypses are open to a spiritual dimension, these typically preserve a dualism that was not entirely characteristic of Jewish and Christian apocalyptic imagination. The recovery of a deeper and broader apocalyptic imagination provides us with a richer perspective on and vocation for technology.

3. Wright, *History and Eschatology*, 57–58.
4. Wright, *History and Eschatology*, 121, 132, 156, 190, 197, 201.

The Cities of the Apocalypse

The Apocalypse of John is explicitly presented as an apocalypse in its first verse or title, along with the divine, human, and artifactual chain of witnesses mediating its content:

> The apocalypse of Jesus Christ,
>> which God gave him to show to his servants what must happen soon.
> He made it known by sending his messenger to his servant John,
>> who witnessed to all that he saw:
>> the word of God, which is the witness of Jesus Christ.
> Blessed is the one who reads aloud and those who hear the words of this prophecy
> and keeps what has been written in it, for the time is near. (1:1–3)[5]

This apocalypse is from and about God and Christ, facilitated through a messenger (*angelos*), received by John, and reduced to writing to be heard and obeyed.[6] John, the self-identified writer of the Apocalypse, shares a vision of the risen Christ (which includes the fusion of two apocalyptic figures from Daniel 7), who instructed him to write what he has seen, "what is, and what is to take place after this" (1:19).

The first part of the Apocalypse consists of seven pastoral letters to seven churches in seven cities in Roman Asia Minor—in Ephesus, Smyrna, Pergamum, Thyatira, Sardis, Philadelphia, and Laodicea (chapters 2–3). In these letters, presumably shared collectively with these and other first-century churches, John communicates messages that address unique conditions in each church and city. Each letter begins with a quality or image of Christ, and each ends with a promise or image of the future. With these remembered and anticipated assurances in view, John commends those who are doing good works in their cities, consoles those who suffer for good works in hostile cities, critiques those whose works are complicit with evil practices and powers, and chastises the complacent whose works are worthless. He also encourages continuing attention to Christ's word and formative practices, including remembrance and repentance, faithful instruction and witness, and patience endurance.

John next shares a series of visions unveiling God's present, past, and coming transformative work in the world and God's true sovereignty. Jesus

---

5. All translations from Revelation are mine.

6. "Keeping" has both attentional and agentic implications. See deSilva, *Discovering Revelation*, 59.

is seen in heaven, as the Lamb (chapters 4–8, 14), and on earth (chapters 6, 12, 19, 21) establishing the kingdom of God. Throughout John's dynamic narrative, which revisits or recapitulates themes such as Christ's coming and the final judgment, there is an intensifying "tension between what ought to be and what is" until Babylon finally falls and New Jerusalem is fully established (chapters 16–22). As violent as the imagery is in these visions, David deSilva emphasizes the important point "that from beginning to end John encourages only non-violent protest and resistance on the part of his Christian audiences."[7]

While some attempt to read the Apocalypse as a simple sequence of events—evil Babylon falls, then good New Jerusalem arrives—deSilva points out "there are indicators that the movement of the plot is not *entirely* linear, but somewhat more complicated."[8] John announces the descending of New Jerusalem before it is fully revealed (3:12[9]), and Babylon's fall is declared before it is witnessed (11:15; 14:8). These and other nonlinear elements of the John's narrative support a reading of the Apocalypse that sees both cities present in the historical cities named and addressed in the book. Before the ultimate destinies of the doomed falling Babylon and the triumphant arriving New Jerusalem are realized in the narrative, these two cities are revealed to be central figures in a "spiritual topography" that encompasses all cities.[10] As deSilva observes, these "alternative cities and ways of organizing human society emerge not merely as scenes in a sequence but scenes that sit in meaningful juxtaposition one to the other."[11] The message to the churches is to turn their attention away from Babylon, the fall of which is certain, and to participate in the arriving reality of New Jerusalem.

The Falling Babylon

In the Apocalypse, Babylon is Rome—"the great city that rules over the rulers of the earth" (17:18). Most commentators place the writing or final compilation of the Apocalypse during the reign of Domitian (81–96 CE), giving it an important imperial context. While traces of past and present

7. deSilva, *Discovering Revelation*, 103, 144.

8. deSilva, *Discovering Revelation*, 10.

9. Although it is translated variously, the tense is present: "the new Jerusalem, which is coming down out of heaven from my God."

10. Resseguie, "Narrative Features of the Book of Revelation," 41.

11. deSilva, *Discovering Revelation*, 11.

persecutions—as well as expectations of future ones—are witnessed in the Apocalypse, most scholars agree that the text was not created during a time of systematic or widespread persecution. But the hostility of the Apocalypse toward its imperial setting—and the political, economic, and religious activities of the Roman empire—is unambiguous.[12] Indeed, John Collins has called the Apocalypse "the most clearly anti-imperial book in the New Testament."[13]

The Roman empire targeted cities as "useful tools" to advance core imperial activities: policing, managing internal competition, economic extraction, and funding warfare and policing. Some two thousand cities participated in Rome's "vast system of domination," which imposed an administrative network over a preexisting regional network of cities.[14] Local civic leaders sustained the Roman tributary empire by collecting revenue and maintaining order, a form of collusion that allowed them to retain some autonomy and prosperity, and they and their cities were rewarded by their imperial rulers. Ephesus, Smyrna, and Pergamum, in particular, enjoyed prosperity and peace under Roman rule. Those who threatened this system—such as early Christians, who confessed allegiance to another sovereignty—threatened the urban foundation of the empire as well as local civic identities.

In the cities of the empire, temples, statues, and coins asserted the glories of Roman prosperity, peace, and power. But John presents his readers and hearers with an alternative narrative about Rome, contradicting those heard in Virgil's *Aeneid* and other works reflecting imperial ideologies. John reveals the inequities and injustices of Rome's prosperity, which exploited many workers—including numerous slaves, who John emphasizes are "human lives"—for the luxurious living of the most powerful (18:13). The peace of the Roman empire, *Pax Romana*, involved systematically killing and enslaving people to secure territories, stabilize economies, and eliminate those who impeded imperial ends. Ultimately, these ends focused on the accumulation of materials goods in Rome. The scale of suffering for which the empire was responsible was significant. Thus John says Rome was inebriated with "the blood of the witnesses to Jesus" and "the blood of the prophets and of the holy ones, and of all who have been slain on earth" (17:6, 18:24). Finally, Rome's belief in its eternal destiny—"*Roma*

---

12. See Friesen, "Apocalypse and Empire," 163.

13. Collins, *Apocalyptic Imagination*, 349.

14. Woolf, *Life and Death of Ancient Cities*, 243.

aeterna"—will be proven false, even if its temporal end is not yet (in the first century) evident. John's indictments and images of economic exploitation, political violence, and ideological hubris uncover the lies of Rome, the "sorcery" by which "all nations were deceived" (18:23). The Apocalypse reveals Rome's true nature: it as an "anticity" of illicit relationships and its empire is a "counterfeit society."[15]

History affirms that all human kingdoms and empires—all aggregations of subjected territories—fall. Drawing heavily form the prophetic traditions in the Hebrew Bible, which denounced older empires such as the commercial empire of Tyre and the historic Babylonian empire, John links the ends of empires with God's judgment. The same end and judgment have come upon Rome, and extend to any empire that aspires to succeed it. Beyond its immediate reference to Rome, the Apocalypse includes a broader critique of any imperial system that seduces rulers and followers with material comforts, that seeks its own power and prosperity at the expense of others, that suppresses opposition, that upholds its survival as the ultimate value, and that is doomed to fail for its denials of what truly sustains life.[16] As Steven Friesen points out, John's critique of Rome makes "his opposition to imperial power systemic enough to be seen as opposed to any empire."[17] And beyond formal empires, John's robust critique can be applied to any oppressive system that dehumanizes, exploits, and subordinates others through economic, political, religious, or ideological practices.

When Babylon fully falls at the climax of John's narrative, its end is celebrated—for its exposed injustices, and its deceptions that convinced so many that such evils were good, are condemned and come to an absolute end. The destruction of Babylon is also lamented. The rulers, merchants, and sea traders who benefited from the excesses of empire lament their loss of power and prosperity. But there is also lament over the loss of cultural activities and artifacts that fill daily life: musicians playing instruments; artisans or artificers of every technical trade working with tools; millers grinding grain; and people lighting lamps and celebrating marriages (18:22–23). These good things, entangled with the collapsing imperial system, will need to find a new life in a new city.

15. Resseguie, "Narrative Features of the Book of Revelation," 43; deSilva, *Discovering Revelation*, 146.

16. See Gorman, *Reading Revelation Responsibly*, 145–46.

17. Friesen, "Apocalypse and Empire," 169.

The Arriving New Jerusalem

The Apocalypse culminates with a vision of "the holy city, the New Jerusalem," coming down from the new heaven to the new earth (21:2). This final city, from and filled with the glory of God, has been prepared for God's people; the names of their tribes and apostles are inscribed on its gates and foundations. The city is an immense cube, constructed out of earthly materials, and possesses a material splendor trivializing any glory of which a human city could boast.[18] The shape of the city alludes to the dimensions of the holy of holies in the Solomonic temple in Jerusalem, but New Jerusalem has no temple—nor does it need any natural or artificial light—for God's presence fills the city and Christ enlightens it. The throne of God has moved from heaven to earth, and from it flows "the river of the water of life." The river runs through the middle of the street, feeding the "tree of life" and its leaves "for the healing of the nations" (22:1–2). In this "new, improved, urban Eden," God and nature fill the city with beauty, life, and healing.[19]

The rulers of the earth and people from all nations—refugees freed from the rule and deceptions of Babylon, drawn by the light of Christ—bring into the New Jerusalem "the glory and the honor of the nations" (21:26). David Aune points out these glories and honors may refer to material gifts and goods, and J. Richard Middleton argues these include "the best of human workmanship that has been developed throughout history . . . human contributions to the new Jerusalem should not be downplayed."[20] Moreover, since technical trades and their technologies were an "essential feature" of ancient cities—including "metalworking, brick-making, glass-making, carpentry, perfume-making, tent-making, spinning, weaving, tanning, dyeing, pottery-making, carving, sculpture, and stonemasonry"—it is easy to imagine certain trades and tools among these gifts and goods.[21] Humanity's "desire to build out of nature a human place of human culture and community" is fulfilled, and there is "perfect harmony between civilization and nature."[22] New Jerusalem presents an image of divine,

18. New Jerusalem is twelve hundred times larger than the ancient city of Babylon as it was measured by Herodotus. See Thomas, *Apocalypse*, 645.

19. Blount, *Revelation*, 395.

20. Aune, *Revelation 17–22*, 1173; Middleton, "New Earth Perspective," 87.

21. Aune, *Revelation 17–22*, 1009.

22. Bauckham, *Theology of the Book of Revelation*, 135; Jürgen Moltmann, quoted in Cosden, *Theology of Work*, 173.

natural, human, and even artificial agency reconciled, brought into proper relationships with each other, and given a new coinherent dynamism.

Brian Blount emphasizes the concrete realism of John's vision of New Jerusalem as "a tangible, measurable, objective city."[23] The eschatological life envisioned in this urban environment includes diverse people and vocations, interdependent and collaborative relationships, and cultural activities and artifacts that constitute the dynamics of civic life. The previously ambiguous image of the city is not annihilated but rather amplified—it continues, transformed, and is the central place of dwelling in new creation where proper relationships are realized with God, oneself, others, the environment, and human creations. The evils of Babylon—the suffering, violence, and injustices on which the empire depended—have been replaced with a different type of ruler and rule, a kingdom of permanent wholeness, peace, and justice. In John's apocalyptic imagination, this is the ideal society toward which human aspirations should be oriented and against which they will be judged.

When John first sees New Jerusalem, Christ—fully revealed as the "ruler of rulers" and the one "who created all things"—declares: "Behold, I am making all things new" (1:5; 4:11; 21:5). While this statement primarily refers to the full and final transformation of reality, commentators point out the present tense "suggests that God is continually making things new here and now."[24] There is another urban network permeating Rome's, and John's readers and hearers are "part of and participant in the new creation, the holy city in which God is ruling." Images of New Jerusalem, Eugene Peterson observes, "are a means for discovering the real" city in present cities, and uncovering the deceptions and distortions of the anticity Babylon.[25]

Participating in the Two Cities

John's overall message to the churches in the Apocalypse is to turn their attention and redirect their agency away from the diabolical and doomed Babylon and toward the present reality and manifestations of New Jerusalem. New creation has begun and is happening now: "The kingdom of the world has become the kingdom of our Lord and of his Christ" (11:15).

23. Blount, *Revelation*, 20.
24. Metzger, *Breaking the Code*, 129.
25. Peterson, *Reversed Thunder*, 183.

The "end is already shaping the present," and the present must be understood with the end in view.[26] God's people, who have been liberated to be "a kingdom," are called to "come out" of the anticity and not participate in its evil works (1:6; 18:4). They are called to remember the witness of Christ (2:5; 3:3), change their ways (2:5, 16, 22; 3:3, 19), and do good and right works—works of "love, faith, service, and patient endurance" (2:19)—that participate in new creation (2:5, 23; 3:2, 15). While John describes Babylon as unambiguously evil, "mother" of the earth's abominations (17:5), John sees the transformation of the human city "as part of God's *good* creation and as the locus of God's grand re-creation." "God is taking what is old and transforming it," Blount observes: "The old will remain a constituent part of the new."[27] Unlike Hesiod's distinct just and unjust cities, the good city of God is present within the evil human city.[28] Thus Augustine claimed, "One part of the earthly city has been made into an image of the Heavenly City."[29]

The Apocalypse provides an "apocalyptic adjustment" to its readers' perception of reality, presenting criteria for discerning and doing what is good and right. Emphasizing the diagnostic over the predictive power of the Apocalypse, deSilva concludes that John calls all of his readers "to do, in their present context, precisely what John sought to do in his own: to discern what is Babylonish about the domination systems in the midst of which they live and of which they themselves may be a part." Identifying and critiquing economic, political, and social injustices is the first step, but this must be followed with alternative practices and courses of action. Some of these actions concern separation from and resistance against current systems: "John knew long before the modern prophets of postcolonialism that one cannot benefit from the exploitive oppression of imperialism without being guilty also of its injustices," deSilva observes, so faithful witnesses must "discover the ways in which they can both divest themselves of participating in and bear prophetic witness against the same." Resistance against should be accompanied with actions for alternative systems: followers of Jesus should "form a vision for human community reflective of God's

26. Boring, *Hearing John's Voice*, 47.

27. Blount, *Revelation*, 376–77.

28. See Hesiod, *Hesiod I*, 107.

29. Augustine, *Concerning the City of God*, 597. Emiliano Rubens Urciuoli points out that the *City of God* "is only nominally a book about cities." Augustine's "restrained" "apocalyptic imagination" does not engage with the "spatial imagination" of the Apocalypse of John. See "Tale of No Cities," 18, 42–44. According to Ando, Augustine is more interested in citizenship than cities. See "Children of Cain," 52.

desires for people . . . to desire a better future, a more just future, a future more reflective of the prophets' vision, Jesus' vision, the apostles' vision, God's vision for human community."[30]

John's message concerns a comprehensive response to the reality and responsibility revealed in Christ. At a macro level, there is a call to align attention and agency with New Jerusalem. John also had more specific messages for churches relating to their unique and local situations, many of which may seem to modern readers more cryptic than apocalyptic—especially about involvement in cultural activities connected with local gods and the imperial cult, which were integrated thoroughly into city life. But these activities were connected with systems of political oppression, and the admonition against participation in such unjust systems never ceased being relevant—particularly when Christians gained imperial and other institutional powers. For all churches, from the first century into the present, strategies of resilience and resistance have included interpreting and preaching Scripture, repentance and praying, teaching and reading, and persevering in acts of faith, hope, and love unto death. In every situation, this involves living into what might and ought to be while confronting what is and should not be.

Christianity spread rapidly throughout the cities of the Roman empire because it improved lives in them. Christian created social services where there were none—caring for the sick, orphans, widows, the elderly, the poor, and addressing many of the miseries of life in the empire.[31] Christianity also developed "in latent conflict" with the Roman empire, "constraining and challenging" its power even after it gained some of that power. By the time they were recognized by Constantine, Christians had created substantial and well organized urban communities and institutions with their own autonomy. And, in time, the Roman Babylon did fall; and Christians, through medieval monastery libraries, preserved many of its important texts. Walter Scheidel argues that the Roman empire and its would-be imperialistic successors demonstrated over the following centuries that "empire, as a way of organizing people and resources, consistently failed to create conditions that enabled transformative development." Roman rule inhibited the development of local governing systems, preventing them from "forming and building a different world." The competitive fragmentation of power that

---

30. deSilva, *Discovering Revelation*, 147, 166, 195–96.

31. See Stark, *Cities of God*, 30, 189.

followed the fall of the Roman empire "ushered in an age of open-ended experimentation" and "a collective release into an unexpected future."[32]

Although imperialistic ambitions mutate and persist—in, for example, modern colonial and commercial enterprises—the Apocalypse and history point to the limits of the imperial imagination: its inability to see, and a hostility against, change and alternate futures. With an imagination constrained by a preference for the status quo, empires and imperialistic systems fail to see the internal and external forces at work that will lead to their ends. Empires are vulnerable to forces outside of their control, such as food shortages, plagues, fire, floods, and earthquakes (all of which are included in the Apocalypse). But they are also vulnerable to internal disruptions that may seem minor or are missed entirely. Christians were a small minority among the many who suffered under Roman rule, and yet Rome became Christian. Christian witness, inspired by the new creation narrative of the Apocalypse—which informs, forms, and transforms—continues to participate in the realization of God's kingdom by separating evil from good and participating in righting a world full of deception and injustice.

Reading the Apocalypse through the lens of African American culture and the tradition of the Black church, Blount claims "John does expect that human believers play a role in the execution of God's eschatological plan" by being a faithful witness. To be a witness, Blount says, is "a call for active, nonviolent resistance." The Greek work for witness, "martyr," now mostly has the connotation of dying for a cause—largely due to the fact that Jesus and many of his followers died because of their powerful witness. In the first century, however, bearing witness described a legal activity—a prophetic or "provocative testimony that had to be given." In the Black church, responding "to the racially charged context that conceived it and gave it birth," faithful witness involves preaching "a message about equality before God" and demanding "that this spiritual reality acquire concrete communal expressions," politically and socially.[33]

As the industrialization and commercialization of American life was accelerating in the early twentieth century, W. E. B. Du Bois lamented how "the question of cash and the lust for gold" had eclipsed "the Preacher and Teacher," who in "the Black World . . . embodied once the ideals of this people,—the strife for another and a better and juster world."[34] Martin Lu-

---

32. Scheidel, *Escape from Rome*, 16, 18–19, 314.

33. Blount, *Can I Get a Witness?*, 39, 42, 47.

34. Du Bois, *Souls of Black Folk*, 418–19.

ther King Jr., who praised Du Bois's "divine dissatisfaction with all forms of injustice" at a centennial celebration of his birth on February 23, 1968, was an embodiment of Du Bois's Black Preacher and Teacher.[35] In a sermon delivered in 1954, King spoke of John's vision of a world being made new:

> John could talk meaningfully about the new Jerusalem because he had experienced the old Jerusalem with its perfunctory ceremonialism, its tragic gulfs between abject poverty and inordinate wealth, its political domination and economic exploitation. John could see this old Jerusalem passing away and the new Jerusalem coming into being.

Babylon, which had conquered Jerusalem both politically and spiritually many times, "did not represent the permanent structure of the universe," King said: it "represented injustice and crushing domination." New Jerusalem, alternatively, represents "justice conquering injustice." "Today," King continued, "we stand between the dying old and the emerging new." The old Babylonian order, with which the church became entangled, included imperialism, colonialism, segregation, and discrimination. "Ultimately history brings into being the new order to blot out the tragic reign of the old order," he concluded. But, King added, "Notice one other point of the text. It mentions that this new city descends out of heaven from God rather than ascends out of earth from man."[36] The ultimate work is God's. In his last speech—"a powerful stream-of-consciousness narrative" and "a powerful spiritual transformation of an earthy situation into a transcendent religious moment"—delivered on April 4, 1968, the night before his assassination, King said:

> It's all right to talk about the new Jerusalem, but one day, God's preacher must talk about the new New York, the new Atlanta, the new Philadelphia, the new Los Angeles, the new Memphis, Tennessee. This is what we have to do.[37]

Every city is a technology and depends on increasingly complex technologies. Some technologies should and will be condemned for their deformative role in patterns of Babylonian counter-creation, and destroyed with the final fall of the old city. Other technologies, participating in the life

---

35. Williams, "M. L. King's Abiding Tribute to W. E. B. Du Bois," 143.

36. King, "Vision of a World Made New," in *Papers of Martin Luther King, Jr., Volume VI*, 182–84.

37. King, "I've Been to the Mountaintop," in *A Call to Conscience*, 201, 214.

of the new city, are transformative and may be among "the glory and the honor of the nations" that find a permanent place in New Jerusalem. If our technologies—including our newest complex artifacts such as autonomous artificial agents—may not be condemned as agents of counter-creation, they may be glorified as agents of new creation.

Technologies of New Creation

The Apocalypse can inform our thinking about—and transform our use of—technology in at least three distinct but interrelated ways. First, it can affirm an ethical minimum for assessing and responding to the impacts of actual and imagined technologies, especially concerning political, economic, and social justice. Second, the Apocalypse points to strategies and structures for resisting and reforming unjust systems and technologies. Third—and most important for inspiring and sustaining ethical reflections and strategic interventions—the vision of the ultimate city of Apocalypse can help us imagine a better world that is not only a future promise but an emerging present actuality.

Apocalyptic ethical commitments and strategies may be found in many contemporary technological critiques and forms of activism. For example, in *Race After Technology: Abolitionist Tools for the New Jim Code*, Ruha Benjamin explores how technologies are often presented "as objective, scientific, or progressive," which hides how they "too often reinforce racism and other forms of inequity." "By pulling back the curtain," Benjamin reveals unjust social dimensions of technology and draws attention to "forms of coded inequity." This awareness enables us "to work together against the emergence of a digital caste system that relies on our naivety" about the seeming neutrality and inevitability of technology.[38] Technologies, designed for specific ends, are not neutral but inherit human agentic intentions and possibilities: the weapons of the industrial age, from the machine gun through the atomic bomb, were designed for mass death. And technologies are not inevitable: they are artifacts created by us and we are responsible for them.

Benjamin identifies four ways inequity is encoded in technologies. When we are not attentive to past patterns of inequity, these are reinforced and amplified by "default discrimination." If non-white people were

38. Benjamin, *Race After Technology*, 1, 6, 100.

prevented from living in a certain part of a city in the past through restrictive covenants, and the less desirable areas where they were allowed to live were "redlined" or judged too risky for bank loans and insurance policies, an automated predictive model using historical data for financial decisions may continue to discriminate against people in that area. As Benjamin puts it succinctly: "racialized zip codes are the output of Jim Crow policies and the input of New Jim Code practices." Inattention to past patterns can also result in "engineered inequity." For example, when language processing models designed to interact through chatbots or suggest content are trained using historical texts that include racist, misogynistic, and other derogatory language, they will recycle this language.[39]

Inattention to the future impacts of technology can lead to encoding new inequities. Benjamin points to "coded exposure," which renders racial groups "hypervisible and expose[s] them to systems of racial surveillance." A fourth form of coded inequity occurs when we are inattentive to present social dynamics and seek technological solutions—"technological benevolence"—to fix different types of bias without considering the systemic social structures that will continue to perpetuate these. Rather than the "revolutionary" fixes promised and pitched by technology companies, Benjamin says what "we urgently need" (quoting Eddie Glaude Jr.) is a "revolution of value and radical democratic awakening." "Amid so much suffering and injustice," Benjamin says, "we cannot resign ourselves to this reality we have inherited. It is time to reimagine what is possible." We also need forms of technological resistance and "abolitionist tools," which require thinking beyond coding.[40]

Philip Butler points to the importance of technology for "Black revolution and liberation." He warns of "the onset of a looming technocratic rule": "The United States is on the cusp of another shift in oppressive structural stratification." "The impending technocracy, which is currently taking shape, is mostly white and mostly male" and "has the ability to reify socially oppressive structures through automation."[41] "Black thriving in near and distant time periods" must be normalized, but "[m]ainstream futuristic depictions are fraught with extravagant designer technologies, ecological possibilities, and scientific exploration that often exclude, relegate, or

39. Benjamin, *Race After Technology*, 24–25.
40. Benjamin, *Race After Technology*, 1, 68, 106, 109.
41. Butler, *Black Transhuman Liberation Theology*, 5, 139, 140.

invisibilize Blackness into irrelevance/obscurity or extinction."[42] This is why Butler founded Seekr, a conversational AI "that is intentionally Black and grounded in spirituality." Seekr normalizes Black experiences, forms of knowledge and imagination, authority, and vernacular.[43]

In his analysis of the colonial foundations of the American university, K. Wayne Yang explains how technologies of colonization create a structural agency that can be used to transform the university into a decolonizing institution. Working with the concept of a cyborg, or a technologically enhanced human being, Yang focuses on the institutional technologies that shape us—that make us "cyborgs . . . plugged in to technological grids." Although universities may begin and exist to perpetuate "imperialist dreams of a settled world," through prescriptive curricula and policies, they cultivate forms of individual and collective agency in learners that can be used to reassemble imperial technologies for alternative futures.[44]

Focusing on Indigenous and Black histories, Yang describes a movement within present universities that is both a rejection of present powers and an affirmation of a deeper wisdom and sovereignty of another world. Like the city, the university is a set of technologies. And, like all technologies, these are teleological or designed for particular ends. Understood this way, it is possible to figure out and forecast how these systems will operate—and then to develop subversive strategies. Against the force of "settler futurity, which is always nostalgic for its current power," technologies can be appropriated for radical transformative projects. These projects are neither dystopian nor utopian: they turn away from imperial fears and false hopes about technology, and recognize that the technologies integrated into our lives can be used to realize a better world.[45]

The ethical critiques and technological strategies of Benjamin, Butler, and Yang, inspired by excluded wisdom and oriented toward new imagined futures, resonate with the moral imagination of the Apocalypse that condemns all forms of oppression and calls for strategic activism to realize "a better and juster world." These penultimate concerns for attention and agency are connected with ultimate ends or *teloi*—which, in the language of Christianity, concern the full establishment of the city and kingdom of

42. Butler, "Introduction," 3.

43. Butler, "Beyond the Live and Zoomiverse," 163. See https://www.theseekrproject.com/.

44. Yang, *Third University Is Possible*, xv, 60.

45. Yang, *Third University Is Possible*, 43.

God. This ultimate *telos* compels action in the present. As Dietrich Bon-hoeffer wrote, summarizing Matthew 25: "The hungry person needs bread, the homeless person needs shelter, the one deprived of rights needs justice, the lonely person needs community, the undisciplined one needs order, and the slave needs freedom." Bonhoeffer noted, however, that there is more to the Christian ethical vision: "The place that in all other ethics is marked by the antithesis between ought and is, idea and realization, motive and work, is occupied in Christian ethics by the relation between reality and becoming real . . . The question of good becomes the question of participating in God's reality revealed in Christ."[46] While apocalyptic criticisms and strategies related to social and structural concerns may seem more relevant to current ethical discussions about technology, the Apocalypse's ultimate concerns for attention and agency may also profoundly enrich many modern manifestations of the apocalyptic imagination that animate current ethical discussions.

46. Bonhoeffer, *Ethics*, 3.

4

||||||||||||||||||||||

Technological Apocalypses

A lthough it describes an ultimate end that seemed near in the first century, the Apocalypse of John has been a resource for the eschatological imagination for nearly two millennia. Many focus on temporal or "horizontal eschatological concerns," which often lead to apocalyptic prophecies that connect promised ends with present circumstances. Others, focusing on more spiritual or "vertical" interpretations of the Apocalypse, create visionary literature such as Dante's *Divine Comedy*.[1] Then there are those who, like Thompson, find nonreligious inspiration from it since the Apocalypse, and the apocalyptic imagination more broadly, "is born of fears and hopes that are endemic to the human condition."[2] Diverse approaches to and uses of the apocalyptic imagination—especially during the twentieth century—have shaped our social and technological imagination.

Recognizing the limits of knowledge—of fully knowing history, others' experiences, ultimate reality and values—Du Bois explored the "artistic imagination" in his proto-Afrofuturist fictional works, sought the inclusion of the "excluded wisdom" of others, and pursued political activism. When we talk about "ultimate reality and the real essence of life and the past and the future," he said, "we seem to be talking without real data." Nevertheless, we must go beyond "objective information": "There is, for instance, faith in the triumph of good deeds; hope that the world will grow better; love of our relatives and our neighbors and of all humanity. It would be difficult

1. Collins, *Apocalyptic Imagination*, 354.
2. Collins, "What Is Apocalyptic Literature?," 13.

to adduce scientific proof that these hopes and faiths are justified, and still there is good reason for our assuming that they are and guiding our conduct accordingly."[3]

In 1938, turning to the apocalyptic imagination to inspire social transformation, Du Bois delivered a commencement address at Fisk University titled "The Revelation of St. Orgne the Damned." Modeling his address on the Apocalypse, Du Bois transformed himself into an apocalyptic Black Preacher and Teacher who had seen the "Seven Stars of Heaven" through the "Seven Heights of Hell"—through birth and family, school and learning, university and wisdom, work, right and wrong, the freedom of art and beauty, and the democracy of race. St. Orgne's experiences, drawn from autobiographical details of Du Bois's life, reveal divine indictments of racial and economic injustice as well as "a sacred plan" including social, educational, economic, religious, cultural, and political reforms that "would foster the creation of a 'new heaven and a new earth.'"[4]

The apocalyptic imagination has also influenced many interested in technological transformation. In *Apocalyptic AI: Visions of Heaven in Robotics, Artificial Intelligence, and Virtual Reality*, Robert Geraci explores the influence of the apocalyptic imagination on influential AI researchers such as Ray Kurzweil, who "have become the most influential spokespeople for apocalyptic theology in the Western world." Their view of apocalypticism "resolves a fundamentally dualistic worldview through faith in a transcendent new realm occupied by radically transformed human beings." They "promise that in the very near future technological progress will allow us to build supremely intelligent machines and to copy our own minds into machines so that we can live forever in a virtual realm of cyberspace." Geraci argues that these views "come directly from Jewish and Christian apocalyptic theology; they are the continuation of those theological traditions."[5] It is worth considering how current uses of the apocalyptic imagination have diverged from—and might reconverge with—the historical and biblical apocalyptic imagination.

3. Williams, "M. L. King's Abiding Tribute to W.E.B. Du Bois," 141–49.

4. Blum, *W. E. B. Du Bois*, 59.

5. Geraci, *Apocalyptic AI*, 8.

American Apocalyptic

Apocalyptic books, films, and thinking have become commonplace in the twenty-first century. Mostly of the "end-of-world-as-we-know-it" variety, these exhibit a range of "doomsday fears—economic, ecological, pestilential, cosmological"—all of which are mingled with technological concerns.[6] Before the mid-twentieth century, however, the apocalyptic imagination was less dominant in the popular imagination. There are important exceptions, such as Mary Shelley's *The Last Man* (1826) and the silent film *Metropolis* (1927). These are among the earliest apocalyptic novels and films connected with the industrial revolutions, and they provide a glimpse of future apocalyptic works to come.

The last man in *The Last Man* is the sole survivor of a global plague in the twenty-first century, and he must console himself with the remaining books and libraries "glowing with imagination and power." "I will not live among the wild scenes of nature," he says; "I will seek the towns—Rome, capital of the world, the crown of man's achievements. Among its storied streets, hallowed ruins, and stupendous remains of human exertion." To the literary record of humanity, the last man adds the last book, his own, dedicated "to the illustrious dead."[7] The last man's world is really the world of *Frankenstein: Or, the Modern Prometheus*—published in 1818, the year in which the fictional translator discovered the last man's record on the prophetic leaves of the Sibyl. The scientific discoveries and technological innovations of the late eighteenth and early nineteenth centuries informed and inspired Shelley's depiction of the new Prometheus Victor Frankenstein, who with a new form of dangerous fire creates a living creature. But Frankenstein creates without love and recapitulates a loss of paradise.[8] The first industrial revolution powered by water and steam was changing the world, and industrial technologies were shaping the technological imagination. The last man laments:

> Farewell to the giant powers of man—to knowledge that could pilot the deep-drawing bark through the opposing waters of shoreless ocean,—to science that directed the silken balloon through the pathless air,—to the power that could put a barrier to mighty

6. Ditommaso, "Apocalypticism and the Popular Culture," 77.

7. Shelley, *Last Man*, 4, 235, 335, 339.

8. Prometheus ("forethought") is the Titan god who gave fire to humans. See Charles E. Robinson, "Introduction," in Mary Shelley, *Frankenstein*, xxviii.

waters, and set in motion wheels, and beams, and vast machinery, that could divide rocks of granite or marble, and make the mountains plain![9]

On the other side of the second industrial revolution of electricity, *Metropolis* presents a less romantic view of technology but a more hopeful apocalypse. Inspired by *Frankenstein* and *R.U.R.*, as well as the role of industrialization in the First World War, *Metropolis* explicitly confronts industrial methods and machinery. Wealthy industrialists rule from the heights of a city—"the new Tower of Babel," with lecture halls, libraries, theatres, stadiums, and "Eternal Gardens"—while underground laborers sacrifice themselves to keep the machinery of the city working. The head and hands are separated, without a heart, and the city waits for a mediator to bring peace. A diabolical inventor creates a robot, the most obedient tool, to destroy the city. It assumes the appearance of Babylon in the Apocalypse, creates discord in the city, and convinces the workers to destroy the machines. The city floods and is subjected to chaos, but at the end a mediator brings the leaders of the industrialists and the workers together at the entrance to the city's cathedral as a new day dawns.[10]

The fear of civilizational decline or collapse—and the loss of accumulated knowledge—is a defining theme in the modern apocalyptic imagination.[11] By the early nineteenth century, it was known that plagues spread through colonization could annihilate vulnerable groups. When George Vancouver voyaged into the lower portion of the inland sea that he would name after his lieutenant Peter Puget in 1792, he noted abandoned homes, human remains along the shorelines, and smallpox scars on those in the Indigenous settlements he visited.[12] The US "empire for liberty" led to more Indigenous deaths, and postapocalyptic literature flourished in the industrializing western US.[13] By the mid-twentieth century, it was clear how industrial technologies had created the condition for global wars. With the invention and demonstration of the atomic bomb, the possibility of nuclear annihilation accelerated the production of works inspired by the apocalyptic imagination.

9. Shelley, *Last Man,* 235.

10. *Metropolis* (1927).

11. See Ditommaso, "Apocalypticism and the Popular Culture," 476.

12. See Cummings, *River That Made Seattle,* 19.

13. Dunbar-Ortiz, *Not "A Nation of Immigrants,"* 19.

Walter Miller's *A Canticle for Leibowitz* (1959), "one of the monuments of science fiction literature," is an example of a postapocalyptic work inspired by the atomic age.[14] After a nuclear "Flame Deluge," enraged survivors destroy what remains of recorded knowledge and technology. Against this "Simplification," Isaac Edward Leibowitz, an engineer-turned-monk, joins a religious order in the American Southwest "to preserve human history" for the descendants of those "who wanted it destroyed." Throughout centuries of cultural darkness, a religious order inspired by Leibowitz keeps a fragmentary record of human knowledge. Even though this information becomes as inscrutable to the monks as it would be to the other inhabitants of their illiterate world, the monks preserve its "symbolic structure" with the hope that one day this information will be analyzed, integrated, and restored—reincarnated in a culture—as applied knowledge. It finally is, during a period of renaissance, and a more advanced civilization emerges. But the pattern of destruction recurs, culminating in another nuclear war, and the order must take its mission of preservation into space, trusting that greater wisdom will, eventually, emerge.[15]

Nuclear technology was not the only new technology contributing to rise of the apocalyptic imagination in the mid-twentieth century: AI, becoming more real than imaginary, began to show up in more books, movies, and television shows. Isaac Asimov began publishing his *I, Robot* short stories in 1942, in which he created laws for robots "that could sense their environment, process information, and act."[16] Kurt Vonnegut's first novel *Player Piano*, published in 1952, imagines a near future world in which machines outperform and displace human work. Early in the novel the protagonist Dr. Paul Proteus refers to Norbert Wiener, whose ideas about automatic control systems "swiftly entered into the public consciousness" through *Cybernetics* (1948) and *The Human Use of Human Beings: Cybernetics and Society* (1950).[17] Proteus explains that if the Industrial Revolution (of steam and then electricity) "devalued muscle work," the next revolution driven by computers (automated and then autonomous) would devalue

14. Ditommaso, "Apocalypticism and the Popular Culture," 495.

15. Miller, *Canticle for Leibowitz*, 62–65, 131, 143–44.

16. The laws are: (1) A robot may not injure a human being or, through inaction, allow a human being to come to harm; (2) A robot must obey the orders given it by human beings except where such orders would conflict with the First Law; (3) A robot must protect its own existence as long as such protection does not conflict with the First or Second Laws. Pasquale, *New Laws of Robotics*, 2–3.

17. Matthews, "'Push-Button Type of Thinking,'" 237.

"routine mental work" and, then, "human thinking"; "thinking machines" would end up doing "the real brainwork."[18]

AI increasingly gained a presence in popular culture during the latter half of the twentieth century, through robots such as Robby, which first appeared in *The Forbidden Planet* (1956) and made subsequent appearances in science fiction movies and television programs, and technologies such as the voice-activated computer in *Star Trek* (1966–69). But postwar pessimism pervaded views about modern technology, and darker visions of technological futures became common. In Stanley Kubrick's *Dr. Strangelove: Or, How I Learned to Stop Worrying and Love the Bomb* (1964), the command and control systems for managing nuclear weapons—heavily dependent on telephones—break down and global nuclear war follows. In Kubrick's next film, Arthur C. Clarke's *2001: A Space Odyssey* (1968), the self-aware computer HAL 9000, which controls the spaceship, malfunctions and becomes murderous. In the 1970 movie *Colossus: The Forbin Project*, based on Dennis Feltham Jones's 1966 novel, control of nuclear defense systems is turned over to an advanced supercomputer. Judging its own intelligence superior to its human creators', it seizes control of the world and promises a future of "peace of plenty and content" under its absolute rule. These and many subsequent AI stories fall into what Ursula K. Le Guin calls the "killer story." This is the "Techno-Heroic" undertaking, "Herculean, Promethean, conceived as triumph, hence ultimately as tragedy." It is the story of the spear, Cain, empire, the bomb, and rogue AI.[19]

As a more popular apocalyptic imagination was emerging during the nineteenth and twentieth centuries, the theological apocalyptic imagination was undergoing a significant change shaped by millennialism. In the twentieth chapter of the Apocalypse, John sees a vision of Christ imprisoning Satan and ruling for one thousand years before the final judgment and end of all evil. One reading of this text expected a historical "pre-millennial" intervention, such as the second coming of Christ, to inaugurate a millennial kingdom. An alternative reading focused more on the historical and/or spiritual millennial progress that would be realized before the full "post-millennial" establishment of the kingdom of God.

In the early nineteenth century, belief in modern and spiritual progress led to a mainstream postmillennial optimism in the United States.

18. Vonnegut, *Player Piano*, 21–22; see Paulus, "Automation and Apocalypse," 177–79.

19. Le Guin, *Always Coming Home*, 728, 30.

According to James Moorhead, Christians "planted one foot firmly in the world of steam engines and telegraph while keeping the other in the cosmos of biblical prophecy."[20] Postmillennialism allowed for "a balance between a progressive view of history and the apocalyptic outlook of the book of Revelation." This led to the creation of new institutions, from benevolent social organizations to ecclesial bureaucracies, and the cultivation of technical knowledge and professional specialization. By the early twentieth century, the "mania for technique, businesslike management, and professional expertise converged in an efficiency movement" epitomized in Frederick Taylor's *Principles of Scientific Management* (1911). Taylor, who expected "an industrial social millennium," preached a "gospel of efficiency" that was adopted by many Protestants. Although focusing on work in the present advanced much good social work, the realized eschatology of many mainstream Protestants "lost the capacity to address humanity's more primal fears and longings and to provide symbols of a transcendent resolution and closure of these issues."[21]

Those looking for a richer eschatology and vision of the end turned to speculative fiction, various forms of premillennialism, and other religious movements that focused on a futurist eschatology. By the end of the twentieth century, the main futurist eschatological tradition in the US was premillennial. More specifically, it was "premillennial dispensationalism," based on a system formulated by John Nelson Darby in the early nineteenth century.[22] Darby is credited with coming up with the idea of the "secret rapture," an event that ends the premillennial period or dispensation, "when Christ will take all true believers into heaven and leave everyone else to suffer a period frequently called the Tribulation." Following this period, Christ is expected "to come yet again, defeat Satan, and inaugurate the Millennium—the reign of Christ on earth."[23] Darby's ideas were codified in *The Scofield Reference Bible* (1909, and revised in 1917) and spread throughout conservative Bible schools, churches, parachurch organizations, and Hal Lindsey's best-selling book *The Late Great Planet Earth* (first published in 1970).[24]

20. Quoted in David Walker Howe, *What Hath God Wrought*, 289.

21. Moorhead, "Apocalypticism in Mainstream Protestantism," 81, 97–98, 103.

22. Collins, *Apocalyptic Imagination*, 356.

23. Frykholm, "Apocalypticism in Contemporary Christianity," 442.

24. The *Left Behind* series of novels (1995–2007) continued the popularization of premillennial dispensationalism.

In addition to other contemporary events, Lindsey pointed to the oppressive possibilities in "our computerized society, where we are all 'numbered' from birth to death." "Leading members of the business community are now planning that all money matters will be handled electronically," he warns, thus making it "possible for people to be controlled economically." But Lindsey was not interested in reforming institutions, not even the church. He was concerned with converting individuals, reducing a statement to one of the churches in the Apocalypse to a call to personal belief: "'Behold, I stand at the door [of your heart] and knock: if any one hears My voice and opens the door, I will come in to him, and will dine [have fellowship] with him, and he with Me' (Revelation 3:20 NASB)."[25]

Collins describes the apocalyptic futurist eschatology popularized by Lindsey and other premillennial dispensationalists as a "highly reductive variant" of the apocalyptic imagination that is "mainly preoccupied with signs of the end." "The literalistic decoding of biblical passages seems simplistic," Collins argues, and is an example of how, "[i]n the hands of literalists, apocalyptic literature distorts human experience and may be ethically dangerous."[26] Lindsey's presentation of apocalyptic eschatology also reveals how the "locus of spirituality among many in the West has shifted, with personal eschatologies replacing institutional ones."[27] Nevertheless, Collins observes, the apocalyptic imagination "is too rich and multiform to be left to the literalists. It is a resilient tradition that continues to haunt our imaginations and remains an indispensable resource for making sense of human experience."[28]

An Apocalypse Remembered

Missing from these popular religious and nonreligious apocalyptic imaginings are visions for positively augmenting knowledge with AI. Shelley's works and the works of her successors suggest loss and danger—a sense of doom shared by dispensationalists such as Lindsey. As AI was entering the popular apocalyptic imagination, information and intelligence automation was becoming a reality. Hopes for transforming the world and our

25. Lindsey, *Late Great Planet Earth*, 113, 186.
26. Collins, *Apocalyptic Imagination*, 356, 358.
27. Ditommaso, "Apocalypticism and the Popular Culture," 503.
28. Collins, *Apocalyptic Imagination*, 358.

understanding of it were growing, although these were left largely to scientists, industrialists, and technocrats to explore. Many of these hopes were represented at the 1962 Seattle World's Fair, which focused on advances in US science and technology. The previous American global exhibition, New York's 1939–40 World's Fair, focused on "Building the World of Tomorrow." The exhibition in Seattle, whose ambitious founders imagined in 1851 that the city would one day be a new New York, similarly focused on the future.[29] Desiring to reflect "the great challenge of life in this atomic and electronic age," planners eventually named the fair the "Century 21 Exposition—America's Space Age World's Fair" to "conjure images of progress."[30] With the launch of the first satellite by the USSR, Sputnik I in 1957, the fair found substantial support from a government eager to promote "the role of science in modern civilization"—which, they hoped, would lead to a more peaceful world.[31] The symbols of the fair—the Space Needle, signifying "soaring and aspiration and progress," and the Monorail (an aerial tramway), signifying "sleek, streamlined, and bold" movement forward—revealed the technological hopes for the time.[32] In their book *The Future Remembered: The 1962 Seattle World's Fair and Its Legacy*, Paula Becker and Alan Stein write that the fair presented "a future ginned up from science-fiction mystique mixed with cutting edge science."[33] The fair also could be described as an apocalyptic event.

The vision for Century 21, recorded in the fair's commission minutes, was to provide "a foretaste of the world to come, rather than a record of the world as it has been."[34] The world to come had to be grounded in the present popular world, though, and one fair advisor warned: "Amusement attractions bring people to the fair. People will not come voluntarily for the educational factors."[35] So the saucer in the Space Needle included a revolving restaurant, and the fairgrounds included the Gayway, with rides and

29. The initial name non-native settlers chose for what would become Seattle was "New York Alki." "Alki," from the Chinook Jargon, means "eventually" or "by and by." See Thrush, *Native Seattle*, 30.

30. Morgan, *Century 21*, 53, 60.

31. Morgan, *Century 21*, 86; see Becker and Stein, *Future Remembered*, 21–22.

32. Morgan, *Century 21*, 136.

33. Becker and Stein, *Future Remembered*, 9.

34. Quoted in Becker and Stein, *Future Remembered*, 24.

35. Morgan, *Century 21*, 13.

games, and "the gaudy and slightly naughty" Show Street.[36] (The fair's largest and most lavish nightclub, the Las Vegas-style Paradise International, used "the apple tree in Paradise" as the symbol for its showgirl revue to "save the fair from science."[37]) But these spectacles were sideshows, and Show Street was largely a financial failure. One consultant warned about "overplaying" the central attraction, the Science Pavilion sponsored by the US government, which was "the largest scientific exhibit ever assembled." "The kind of figures people come to fairs to see," he asserted, "aren't fed into computers." But most fairgoers—6.8 out of 9.6 million attendees—visited the Science Pavilion, and more people returned to it for a second visit than any other display.[38]

The Science Pavilion, in a "space gothic complex" surrounding a reflecting pool, oriented visitors to the new "World of Science." An orientation film, *The House of Science*, introduced the exhibition and the primordial ability and desire of the human being "to reach out with the mind and his imagination to something outside himself" and progressively add to the structure of knowledge.[39] Visitors then learned about the growth of science, accelerated with technological developments, and experienced a simulated rocket ride through space in a planetarium (the Spacearium, sponsored by Seattle's largest employer, the Boeing Airplane Company). Fairgoers witnessed scientific demonstrations and learned "how science and technology can be used by society to help broaden mankind's civilization and his future." "In order to make wise decisions," the official souvenir program explained, we must "be aware of science's implications . . . it is not enough to accept the changes. Foresight and planning are necessary." Finally, for younger visitors, there was a hands-on laboratory where they could perform simple experiments. Praising the US exhibit, President Kennedy wrote: "We all must learn more of science. Together with its blessings, science presents us with difficult social questions. These can be answered, not in the laboratory, but in the open discussions of free men aspiring toward a fuller life for all mankind."[40]

The World of Commerce and Industry section of the fairgrounds—especially exhibitors in the US section, which the official program promised

36. *Seattle World's Fair 1962*, 61.

37. Becker and Stein, *Future Remembered*, 52, 138.

38. Morgan, *Century 21*, 13–14.

39. Morgan, *Century 21*, 15.

40. *Seattle World's Fair 1962*, 6.

"reveal the future"—also drew significant crowds. The Hydro-Electric Utilities Display, the Bell Telephone Systems Exhibit, and the US Plywood Association American Home of the Immediate Future each drew about three-and-a-half million visitors. In the Bell exhibit, fairgoers saw "machines 'talking' to machines and future design telephones such as the picture phone, which one day may make it possible to display books, clothing, groceries and even art treasures in your home." In the "three gardens of learning" in the IBM Pavilion, some three million visitors learned about technological accomplishments of the past, how computers operate, and how computers have "added a new dimension to information processing and control" and "some of the ways they may help solve many of the mysteries in the world of tomorrow."[41] And the General Electric Living Exhibit, showing electronic household innovations from an electronic sink and bakery drawer to an electronic home library and home computer, attracted some two million visitors.

At the center of the World of Century 21 section of the fair, housed in the Washington State Coliseum, was the World of Tomorrow exhibit. A spherical elevator called the Bubbleator lifted riders into a honeycomb-shaped cloud that contained a multisensory narrative—with motion pictures, recordings, music, odors, and sound and lighting effects—that was "both hopeful and realistic" about "an easy, gracious, stimulating future." The prologue to the narrative, titled "The Threshold and the Threat," began with the threat: a family waiting for help in a nuclear fallout shelter. Visitors' attentions were called away from this vision, and they progressed down a winding ramp, "guided by intricate electronic programming," through interconnected cubes on which were projected images of future environments—the city, home, office, farm, and school of the future—full of plastics, videos screens, and automation.[42] At the end, the image of the family in the fallout shelter returned and visitors heard Kennedy's voice "calling upon everyone to use the knowledge of the present to build a brighter world of tomorrow—a world free of the threat that clouds the threshold."[43]

Surrounding the World of Tomorrow exhibit were exhibits amplifying predictions of the future in transportation, communication, and other areas. One popular exhibit, visited by nearly two million, was the American Library Association's Library 21. Aiming to demonstrate how libraries were

41. *Seattle World's Fair 1962*, 26, 31, 33.
42. *Seattle World's Fair 1962*, 20.
43. Becker and Stein, *Future Remembered*, 106.

integrating "machines into an environment of books," the exhibit included a UNIVAC (a universal automatic computer), microformats, and other electronic devices. The UNIVAC was used to provide annotated bibliographies on certain topics, "converse" on topics drawn from Mortimer Adler's *Great Books of the Western World* (1952), and provide facts from "gazetteer-type data."[44] The exhibit also included more traditional reference, adult, and children's books, as well as reference and readers' advisory services.

Three buildings represented religion at Century 21. There was a Christian Science Pavilion, providing information about the teachings of Christian Science as well as news from the *Christian Science Monitor*. The Sermons from Science Pavilion provided daily sermons that connected scientific facts with faith. The model for these sermons, developed by Irwin Moon for the Moody Institute of Science, explained scientific discoveries that revealed God's creative power and humans' need for redemption. In "God of the Atom," for example, Moon describes nuclear energy, which "can be a great blessing to humanity or it can destroy us completely." "The choice is life or death," he says, for "the God of the atom, the God of infinite power, is the God of everlasting salvation to whosoever believeth in him."[45] The "major religious presence on the grounds," however, was the Christian Witness Pavilion, situated in a prime location opposite and below the gothic arches of the Science Pavilion.[46] It was "primarily devoted to child evangelism and to helping assuage fear of thermonuclear annihilation with teachings about the hereafter"[47] According to James Gilbert, it "had more success as a day care center and Sunday school for the children of visitors" than as a Christian witness to the significant technological and social issues of the day.[48]

Century 21 occurred in the midst of social crises and existential threats. The rights revolutions of the 1960s and 1970s—the culmination of previous decades of progressive momentum such the "long Civil Rights Movement"[49]—were coming. In 1962, more than 90 percent of Se-

44. Lieberman, "Library 21," 93–94.

45. The Moody Institute for Science was affiliated with the Moody Bible Institute, which was founded by Dwight L. Moody, "who did more than anyone else in America to spread premillennial views of an imminent end" and at the same time made long-term plans for educational institutions. Marty, "Future of No Future," 462.

46. Gilbert, *Redeeming Culture*, 318.

47. Becker and Stein, *Future Remembered*, 116.

48. Gilbert, *Redeeming Culture*, 318.

49. Putnam and Garret, *Upswing*, 227.

attle's population was white, largely due to a hundred years of racist land ownership laws. And during the final days of Century 21, women were prohibited officially from becoming astronauts—even though they had made significant contributions to the US space program. But in 1964 the Civil Rights Act became law, which prohibited discrimination on the basis of race, religion, sex, or national origin. While Century 21 did not focus on these social issues, it did not ignore the existential threat posed by nuclear weapons, and the day after the fair closed the world was reminded of the imminence of this risk. President Kennedy had been scheduled to arrive on the final day of the fair, but then it was reported that he had come down with a cold—and so had Vice President Lyndon Johnson. The day after, Kennedy "unveiled" what came to be known as the Cuban Missile Crisis.[50]

And yet the surprising popularity of science and technology at Century 21, over other figures and spectacles, pointed to the achievements and hopes of the age. The fair made an impression on many, including a number of future scientists and technological entrepreneurs such as Bill Gates and Paul Allen. But while the significance of the time was sensed by all, only in retrospect is the profound nature of the changes underway at the time evident. A central and transformative change—evidenced in Bell's automated phone system, IBM's voice-activated calculator, GE's automated home appliances, and the Library 21 UNIVAC—was the information automation revolution. Soon after the invention of digital computers in the 1940s, mathematicians and engineers had begun working on creating AI technologies. But others began working on a different project: intelligence augmentation. Instead of trying to simulate human intelligence, they worked on technologies that would help humans do intellectual work—technologies that led to the invention of the personal computer and computer networking.[51]

By the 1960s, information-processing technologies were augmenting human industry and knowledge in new and significant ways. Libraries, which had remained largely unchanged for decades, began using computers to automate operations. They also planned for new information resources and networks, and reimagined their roles and work in new information environment.[52] In the 1970s, Marshall McLuhan and Robert Logan observed that the library, "an old figure in a new ground," was repositioning

50. Becker and Stein, *Future Remembered*, 9, 195.

51. See Markoff, *Machines of Loving Grace*, esp. 5–18.

52. See National Advisory Commission on Libraries, "Technology and Libraries," in Kaplan, ed., *Reader in Library Services and the Computer*, 5–10.

itself in a new information environment. As new electronic media entered mainstream library collections, and as librarians began to help people copy and reassemble information with photocopiers and computers, the role of the library was shifting from a more "passive distributor of the information artifacts of others to that of the manufacturer of information on par with a publisher, a filmmaker, or a broadcaster." "[W]e are moving into an age in which information is becoming the prime concern of mankind, the key to survival in a complicated environment," they claimed, and the "challenge facing libraries is to fully exploit the new technologies while at the same time preserving the best of the past traditions of the library."[53]

Libraries were adapting to the new dynamics of the information age, but many other institutions were not preparing for a future being shaped by automated information processing. Automation of work, in particular, began to accelerate in the 1970s. Viewed as an efficient end in itself, instead of a way of augmenting human work, automation increasingly displaced human workers over the following decades.[54] Putnam and Garrett point out that the "interplay between technological advance and the educational innovations (especially the pubic high school) that emerged from the Progressive Era around 1910" was "fine for the assembly lines that dominated economic growth from the 1920s to the 1970s, but is was inadequate for the high-tech labs that replaced those assembly lines into the last decades of the twentieth century."[55]

Seattle and the Technological Imagination

Although it became known as a place of digital innovation in the 1980s, Seattle was not the most obvious place to imagine the technological future in the mid-twentieth century. A few years after the Great Exhibition of the Industry of All Nations in 1851, as the US was expanding westward to realize its own imperial and industrial ambitions, George Whitworth arrived in the new Territory of Washington with the dream of establishing a Presbyterian "colony" in the region. "The people of the United States are great colonizers," he wrote, "and the best elements of effective colonization are intelligence, enterprise, and religion." A booklet celebrating the fiftieth

53. Logan with McLuhan, *Future of the Library*, 4, 77, 81, 180.

54. Siddarth et al., "How AI Fails Us," 5.

55. Putnam and Garret, *Upswing*, 47–48.

anniversary of the first church organized by Whitworth claimed that in 1854 the Pacific Northwest "was almost unbroken wilderness." Fifty years later, it observed, "the beautiful shores of Puget Sound are now adorned with magnificent cities, which have become the gateways of commerce."[56]

In addition to his church-building work for white settlers, Whitworth was a land surveyor, participated in treaty negotiations, developed coal mines, and helped establish schools and universities.[57] In 1907, Whitworth published a retrospective of the "striking events and wonderful changes" that had happened during his decades in Seattle. Whitworth praised steam and electric power, along with steamers, telegraphy, rotary presses, automobiles, trolleys, and trains. All of these technological innovations had transformed the frontier settlement of Seattle from 150 white settlers into a metropolis of nearly a quarter-million denizens—mostly white, due to a series of laws excluding the presence of others. As the US developed from an agrarian country into a global industrial power, Whitworth thought Seattle represented the "Hercules"-like power of the US and the veracity of George Berkeley's statement, "Westward the course of empire takes its way."[58]

Before Seattle was established and shaped by the industrial technological imagination—before early settlers imagined a great city displacing Indigenous people and settlements—there was an Indigenous technological imagination that had created a network of settlements integrated into the natural environment. These represented an altogether different pattern for integrating natural and artificial agency. As David Williams observes, the Indigenous people of Puget Sound

> developed a culture based on coexistence with the region's abundant natural resources. Extended family groups established winter villages, which were the home base and heart of social and ceremonial life. At other times of year they moved to seasonal camps to acquire useful plants and animals. They continuously modified their technologies and strategies to increase their food harvests. In doing so, they created a sustainable and resilient lifestyle based on reciprocity between bands of people inhabiting different watersheds, which persisted up to the time of contact with Europeans.

The treaties that Washington Territorial Governor Isaac Stevens began hastily executing in 1854, which technically transferred Indigenous "right,

---

56. Both sources quoted in Welsh, *Presbytery of Seattle*, xxii.
57. See Drury, "George Frederick Whitworth," 4, 7.
58. Whitworth, "Retrospect of Half a Century," 206.

title, and interest in and to the lands" to the US government (which already had begun distributing the land in 1850), largely ended the Indigenous approach to stewardship of the land. Now, "the land was there to be owned and used"; natural resources were "products to be acquired, processed, and sold." Although the treaties codified this dominant industrial way of relating to the land, Williams points out that they also "codified Native people's right to hunting, fishing, and gathering, which preserved, albeit on the margins," an Indigenous approach to the environment from which we may still learn.[59]

The American settlers and industrialists radically reshaped the landscape and waterways around Seattle, making the Duwamish River—named after the Indigenous people of the place—unrecognizable and one of the nation's most contaminated rivers.[60] This is a common example of how the industrial technological imagination, focused on "the economics of commodity production and the management of resources," creates what Daniel Wildcat describes as "engineered boxes of insulated ignorance." Not "paying attention" to the voices of the land, he warns, results in "murdering the creation of which we are a part."[61] "To reconstruct the world," Le Guin similarly warns, "rather than participating in what is . . . is to run the risk of losing or destroying what in fact is." Those who think they have found a new world—which was known better before it was "discovered"—often find themselves living in a lost world.[62] Ancient wisdom can help us broaden our technological imagination. For example, Randy Woodley argues that "engaging the biblical witness from an Indigenous perspective" can help us understand Jesus's kingdom over against the "rapacious industrial-imperial situation that we live under" now.[63]

Whitworth's observations about Seattle's industrial potential came at a high point for the industrial city. The main exception was the start of the Boeing Airplane Company in 1916. According to Michael Luis, the region's "economy changed little from 1907 to 1967"; into the 1950s, due to its small size and remoteness, the Puget Sound region was not "a suitable location for conventional industry" and relied on "resource-based industries."[64] In

59. Williams, *Homewaters*, 29, 45, 47.

60. See Cummings, *River That Made Seattle*, 174–75.

61. Wildcat, "Enhancing Life in a World of Relatives," 306, 308–9.

62. Le Guin, *Always Coming Home*, 705; see also 701.

63. Woodley, "Early Dialogue in the Community of Creation," 93.

64. Luis, *Century 21 City*, 61–62.

the decade that followed Century 21, Seattle was forced to confront its industrial and imperialist commitments. Suffering from declining government funding and sales in the late 1960s, Boeing shed more than 60 percent of its workforce in just a few years. In 1971, two real estate agents put up a billboard sign that said, "Will the last person leaving SEATTLE—Turn out the lights."[65] In the midst of this economic disruption, local activism began to change the city. On March 8, 1970, more than a hundred Indigenous men, women, and children invaded Fort Lawton, a decommissioned army base in Seattle, and invoked treaties and claimed the fort "by the right of discovery."[66] This performative reversal of what had happened over a hundred years earlier resulted in the creation of the Daybreak Star Indian Cultural Center in 1973.[67] According to Coll Thrush, "By the 1980s, Seattle had become a center of pro-Indian and pro-environment sentiment, perhaps symbolized in the formal apology for cultural genocide and religious oppression that was issued by Seattle-area churches in 1987."[68]

Beginning in the 1970s, computer technologies became mass-market commodities and declining government funding for technological development was increasingly replaced with private financing. Following the arrival of Microsoft in 1979 and Amazon in 1994, the Seattle area became what Margaret O'Mara calls "a city of knowledge." Such cities are "centers of high-tech innovation and productivity, magnets for the professional class, with powerful research universities as their intellectual centers."[69] Today, the Seattle area hosts large teams from Silicon Valley-based companies such as Meta (formerly Facebook) and Google (part of Alphabet), and Amazon's presence in Bellevue, Washington—where Bezos first rented a house with a garage (to access the "garage start-up" mythology of new technology companies)—rivals its presence in Seattle. The future dimly glimpsed and prophesied in Seattle in 1962 is in some ways now being realized.

In an address to the Princeton graduating class of 2010, Bezos explained the source of inspiration for starting Amazon in 1994:

> I came across the fact that web usage was growing at 2,300 percent per year. I'd never seen or heard of anything that grew that fast, and the idea of building an online bookstore with millions

65. Lange, "Billboard Reading."
66. Thrush, *Native Seattle*, 162.
67. See Berger, "Introduction," in Sale, *Seattle*, xxii.
68. Thrush, *Native Seattle*, 190.
69. O'Mara, *Cities of Knowledge*, 232–34.

of titles—something that simply couldn't exist in the physical world—was very exciting to me.[70]

That same year, Amazon began moving into a cluster of new buildings in Seattle's South Lake Union neighborhood and Bezos began to praise the possibilities of AI. In 2013, Brad Stone published a book on Amazon titled *The Everything Store*, which told the story of how one of the first and largest bets on the internet "fought off near ruin and upended not only retail but digital media and enterprise computing." Stone thought he "had written the comprehensive book on Amazon's rise," but it was soon clear the ascent of Amazon was not over. In 2014, Amazon released the voice-activated device Echo, powered by the digital assistant Alexa. The next year it reported the financial results of its cloud computing web services division AWS, "shocking investors with its profitability and growth." By 2020, the everything store had become an AI and cloud company, as well as a robotics manufacturer, Hollywood studio, video game maker, grocery store, and more.[71]

At the apogee of its rise in Seattle, in January 2018 Amazon opened—with Bezos issuing a command to Alexa—the architectural centerpiece of its corporate campus, the Spheres, three interconnected domes housing some forty thousand diverse plants. A month earlier, the *Seattle Times* had reported on a pattern of growth that had paralleled Amazon's and Seattle's prosperity—the rise of homelessness. By December 2017, the Seattle area had the third-largest homeless population in the country. Over eleven thousand people were unhoused, about half of whom were unsheltered and living on the streets or in tents. There were over 4,200 homeless kids in city schools.[72] Because of its growing wealth, power, scale, and impact, Amazon has not only transformed its home city but has become, in Stone's words, "a referendum on society, and on the responsibilities that large companies have toward their employees, their communities, and the sanctity of our fragile planet."[73] Amazon is not the only technology company that has changed our lives and world. But, as Alec MacGillis observes, "in upending how we consumed—the ways that we fulfilled ourselves—it had recast daily life at the most elemental level" in both digital and physical spaces.[74]

70. Bezos, *Invent and Wonder*, 195.

71. Stone, *Amazon Unbound*, 12–14.

72. MacGillis, *Fulfillment*, 212.

73. Stone, *Amazon Unbound*, 2.

74. MacGillis, *Fulfillment*, 11.

As O'Mara points out, while the city of knowledge model "seems to have been very good for productivity, it has had negative social, environmental, and economic consequences." Cities of knowledge cannot "accommodate all who want to live and work in them." Their economic exclusivity drives up the value of land and forces "people and industries to move elsewhere."[75] The future realized sixty years after the vision of Century 21 reveals that we need a knowledge and wisdom revolution to accompany our current industrial and information revolution. Together, AI and the apocalyptic imagination can help with such a revolution.

Apocalypse Now and Not Yet

Whether foretelling events through inspired revelations or forecasting possibilities through natural observations, our species has been future-oriented from the beginning. We exist now and as we do because our ancestors were able to identify future threats and opportunities and then imagine, analyze, and choose preferred alternative actions. Modern approaches to futures thinking often focus on rational and mathematic models, which are now tremendously powerful with the aid of big data and predictive algorithms. But imagining the future has never been reducible to scientific methodologies. The reality is that the apocalyptic imagination, whether described as religious or secular, is more popular than ever. Indeed, in the twenty-first century, as "a response to the magnitude of environmental, economic, and social problems," we have witnessed an "apocalyptic turn" in the popular imagination.[76] This turn intersects with hopes and fears associated with our current information revolution.

Although "apocalyptic" now typically refers to the end of the world— or at least the end of the world as we know it—the apocalyptic imagination continues to provide a conceptual and narrative framework for answering "big questions about space, time, and the purpose of life."[77] Rather than denying or avoiding it, the range of ideas and images inspired by the apocalyptic imagination is worthy of exploration and engagement. But if the apocalyptic imagination is to be a generative resource for imagining and creating a better world and future, it is important to identify some

75. O'Mara, *Cities of Knowledge*, 239.
76. Ditommaso, "Apocalypticism and the Popular Culture," 473, 503.
77. Ditommaso, "Apocalypticism and the Popular Culture," 480.

distinctions among various apocalyptic views to see where shared values may converge.

First, some apocalyptic eschatologies are more religious in nature, believing in a hidden transcendent reality that informs the world, the future, and "gives life meaning and purpose." Others, according to Lorenzo Ditommaso, are more secular and equate transcendent reality "with a divinized humanity, superhuman agencies, a force of nature or history, or anything else that does not require supernatural explanation."[78] As Geraci and others have shown, religious apocalyptic eschatologies have inspired and informed many technological apocalyptic eschatologies.[79]

Second, some apocalyptic eschatologies emphasize continuity between the present and the future and focus more on what has been or can be realized. Whether religious or not, these realized eschatologies emphasize the role and power of human agency in bringing about desired ends. They are more prone to believe, for example, that humans and AI will bring about a better world on their own. Futurist eschatologies, on the other hand, focus on an unrealized future and emphasize discontinuity. These tend to denigrate the world and de-emphasize the ability of human agency to transform it. From this perspective, many conclude that nonhuman agents—divine, natural, or artificial—will destroy the world independently.

Another view of apocalyptic eschatology can be found in cultures that have experienced colonization, forced relocation, slavery, and diaspora in the modern era. For these cultures, "the apocalypse has already happened." Indigenous, African, Asian, Latinx, and other futurisms—often through "a subversive reworking of technology"—imagine alternate worlds where survival is possible.[80] One theme in Indigenous speculative fiction is the value of "Indigenous scientific literacies"—"sustainable forms of medicine, agriculture, architecture, and art"—and techniques that "reenergize the natural environment while improving the interconnected relationships among all persons (animal, human, spirit, and even machine)."[81]

Between realized and unrealized eschatologies is the perspective of an inaugurated eschatology, which is "how the majority of historic and global Christianity has interpreted Jesus's instruction on the Kingdom of God."[82]

78. Ditommaso, "Apocalypticism and the Popular Culture," 474, 479.

79. See Geraci, *Apocalyptic AI*, 8.

80. Sanchez-Taylor, *Diverse Futures*, 10, 20, 23.

81. Dillon, *Walking the Clouds*, 7.

82. Langford, "Theological Framework for Reflection on Artificial Intelligence," 88.

For Christians, this apocalyptic eschatology concerns the past and future work of Christ and how that work is transforming the present. Inaugurated eschatologies acknowledge that the future is being realized in the present, while recognizing that many future hopes have not yet been fully realized, and they tend to emphasize more continuity than discontinuity between the future and the present. Most importantly, an inaugurated eschatology focuses on the role of humans as agents in realizing the future—and it can help us imagine how artificial agency may participate in new creation as well. An inaugurated eschatological perspective can serve as a middle way for realizing human hopes through actions in the present. Across all of these religious and secular apocalyptic views, it is possible to find common agreements on a number of penultimate goals, at least, while acknowledging differences and disagreements about ultimate ends.

5

|||||||||||||||||||||||

Our Information Apocalypse

In 1999, Čapek's apocalyptic robots received a significant upgrade in the artificial agents of the *The Matrix*—a movie about the subjugation of humans by AI. Soon after it came out, I left my office in downtown Seattle early on a gray day to catch a matinee. I did not know anything about the story, and the trailer I had seen did not make much sense to me. But I caught allusions to Jean Baudrillard's notion of hyperreality, when representations of reality have no connection with actual reality—what Las Vegas had become in the 1990s. It was still day when I emerged from the theater, and the familiar skyscrapers surrounding me now seemed strange and ominous.

I had recently finished working on information systems audits related to the so-called Y2K bug, which referred to programs that would confuse 2000 with 1900 due to two-digit year formats, so I thought our real concerns about computer systems were rather mundane. Because of that work, I had come to appreciate how dependent we had become on automated information processing—and that we could tackle society-wide challenges that threatened that dependence. What I had not yet realized was how little I had reflected on the changing and problematic dynamics of the technological society in which I had grown up and was participating.

The protagonist of *The Matrix*, Thomas Anderson, is a computer programmer who lives a secret life as a hacker under the alias Neo. Neo is restless, sensing and seeking a deeper or transcendent reality. His searching leads him to Morpheus, who affirms what Neo knows and feels: "that there is something wrong with the world." Morpheus reveals the hidden truth that Neo and most of humanity is living in a simulation. Morpheus explains,

"At some point in the early twenty-first century, all of mankind was united in celebration. We marveled at our own magnificence as we gave birth to AI . . . A singular consciousness that spawned an entire race of machines." War followed, humans scorched the sky to cut off solar power for the machines, and the machines turned humans into an energy source. The Matrix, a computer-generated dream world and prison for human minds, was "built to keep us under control in order to change a human being into [a battery]." Morpheus observes, "Throughout human history we have been dependent on machines to survive. Fate, it seems, is not without a sense of irony."[1]

In *The Matrix* and the three sequels in the franchise—*The Matrix Reloaded*, *The Matrix Revolutions* (both from 2003), and *The Matrix Resurrections* (2021)—humans and machines battle online and offline for control of the future of the world as they negotiate their mutual interdependence. In the first movie, Neo is initially presented as a savior figure—dying and rising in the Matrix to overcome it. But in the next two films, his role is much more complex: he is part of the machines' plan, meant to reboot the Matrix because it is constantly corrupted by unpredictable human actions. From the beginning, machines could not control human agency. In the first movie, Agent Smith tells Neo, "The first Matrix was designed to be a perfect human world, where none suffered, where everyone would be happy. It was a disaster—no one would accept the program."[2] Both human and artificial agents upset the subsequent plan for the Matrix, and the Machine City and Zion, the last human city, reach a tentative truce in the third movie. In *The Matrix Resurrections*, even more complex relationships have developed between humans and machines: Zion has become Io, and the new Matrix is powered by the love of Neo and the female protagonist of the franchise, Trinity, who empowered Neo's resurrection in the first film. When that love is fully resurrected in the final film, Trinity and Neo are able to redesign the Matrix in whatever way they think best.

Like Čapek's apocalyptic figure of the robot, the agents in *The Matrix* are a synecdoche of technological culture at the turn of the twenty-first century. When the first movie was released in 1999, *Time* magazine named Bezos "Person of the Year" for embodying "e-commerce and dot-com mania."[3] AI was part of the tech stack: IBM's Deep Blue program defeated reigning world chess champion Garry Kasparov in 1997, but this was the only task

1. *Matrix* (1999).
2. *Matrix* (1999).
3. Earle, "Timeline We're On Is Even Darker Than 'The Matrix' Envisioned."

it could perform and it succeeded through "a brute force approach."[4] The main technological threat seemed to be the Y2K bug, and the most important technology was the internet. *The Matrix* trilogy presented a dystopian view of life online when the popular view was much more utopian; it raised questions about our control of this popular new technology and how it would be integrated into our lives. The fourth movie, released nearly twenty years later—when the popular view of the current internet, dominated by social media, has become much more dystopian—provided a much more hopeful view. With more clarity about and care for our condition, the final film suggests we can create a better technological society. But we need to seek greater wisdom to upgrade our technological understanding and formative practices along with our material technologies.

Our Apocalypse

The One Hundred Year Study of Artificial Intelligence (AI100) is a long-term, multidisciplinary investigation of AI "and its influences on people, their communities, and society." The AI100 plan is to convene a study panel every five years to provide "a collected and connected set of reflections about AI and its influences as the field advances" that are of value to the general public, industry, governments, and AI researchers.[5] The first AI100 report, published in September 2016, "influenced discussions on governmental advisory boards and workshops in multiple countries. It has also been used in a variety of artificial intelligence curricula."[6] The report chose as its theme "AI and Life in 2030," and focused on "a typical North American city," acknowledging "the central role cities have played throughout most of human experience." Downplaying "frightening, futurist portrayals of Artificial Intelligence that dominate films and novels, and shape the population's imagination," the report focused on everyday accomplishments including the increasing autonomation of vacuum cleaners, vehicles, healthcare analytics, tutors, surveillance, job tasks, and personalized amusements—and predicted "substantial developments" by 2030.[7]

---

4. Mitchell, *Artificial Intelligence*, 8.
5. Stone et al., "Artificial Intelligence and Life in 2030," 1.
6. Littman et al., "Gathering Strength, Gathering Storms," 1.
7. Stone et al., "Artificial Intelligence and Life in 2030," 2, 6, 49.

"AI and Life in 2030" pointed out challenges with AI, such as safe and reliable hardware for self-driving vehicles and service robots, keeping human experts integrated into healthcare and education, gaining public trust in public safety and security, preventing the marginalization of human work, and protecting interpersonal relationships within an increasingly sophisticated and enticing entertainment ecosystem. But the report emphasized the priority of "encouraging innovation" over regulation: "Rather than 'more' or 'stricter' regulation, policies should be designed to encourage helpful innovation, generate and transfer expertise, and foster broad corporate and civic responsibility for addressing critical societal issues raised by these technologies."[8]

When the second AI100 report appeared in September 2021, popular perceptions of technology had changed dramatically. According to the Pew Research Center, in 2015, 71 percent of Americans thought technology companies were "having a positive effect on the way things are going in the country."[9] By 2019—with growing concerns about digital distractions, deceptions, divisiveness, and dangers—that number had declined to 50 percent.[10] Since then, converging health, economic, racial, political, and climate crises have led to a broader awareness of and more ethical approaches to addressing the social impacts of AI. "The bloom is off the rose of the big tech companies," write Rob Reich, Mehran Sahami, and Jeremy Weinstein in *System Error: Where Big Tech Went Wrong and How We Can Reboot*:

> We no longer hear so much gushing about the internet as a tool for putting a library into everyone's hands, social media as a means of empowering people to challenge their governments, or tech innovators who make our lives better by disrupting old industries. The conversation has shifted to the other pole. Humans are being replaced by machines, and the future of work is uncertain. Private companies surveil in ways that governments never even contemplated and profit handsomely in the process. The internet ecosystem feeds hate and intolerance with its echo chambers and filter bubbles. The conclusion seems inescapable: our technological future is grim.[11]

---

8. Stone et al., "Artificial Intelligence and Life in 2030," 42, 49.

9. Auxier et al., "10 Tech-Related Trends That Shaped the Decade."

10. See Anderson and Rainie, "Future of Well-Being in a Tech-Saturated World."

11. Reich et al., *System Error*, xxiv–xxv.

The contributors to *Your Computer Is on Fire* argue further that we "can no longer afford to be lulled into complacency by narratives of techno-utopianism or technoneutrality, or by self-assured and oversimplified evasion." Thomas Mullaney calls on us to interrogate every "established or emerging norm" in our technological environment and identifies a number of hidden values embedded in current technologies:

> the taken-for-granted whiteness of humanoid robots, the ostensibly "accentless" normative speech of virtual assistants, the near invisibility of human labor that makes so many of the ostensibly "automated" systems possible, the hegemonic position enjoyed by the English language and the Latin alphabet within modern information-processing systems, the widespread deployment of algorithmic policing, the erosion of publicly governed infrastructures at the hands of private (and ultimately ephemeral) mobile platforms, the increasing flirtation with (if not implementation of) autonomous weapons systems capable of selecting and engaging targets independently, and the list goes on.[12]

Mar Hicks claims our current "informational infrastructure is in ruins," and urges us "to take advantage of this moment of disaster" to reflect on and "recognize that technological progress without social accountability is not real progress."[13] Technology "will deliver on neither its promises nor its curses," Benjamin Peters adds; "the flow of history will continue to surprise . . . the world never fails to surprise." But we need to "stop off-loading and outsourcing the imagination of better worlds" to technological solutions; we need to attend to the earth and keep "learning to love, live with, and care for others."[14]

The optimism in AI100's 2016 report for AI's "potentially profound positive impacts" was tempered in AI100's 2021 report, titled "Gathering Strength, Gathering Storms": "We remain similarly optimistic. However, society's broader worries about the future in terms of inequity, discrimination, and our ability to work together to address our most significant global challenges are reflected in concerns about the future of AI." The 2021 report focuses on the "remarkable" progress of AI technologies over the last five years, but also on the impact AI is having "on people and societies worldwide" now. Areas of notable progress include: natural language processing,

12. Mullaney, "Your Computer Is on Fire," 4–5.
13. Hicks, "When Did the Fire Start?," 22–23.
14. Peters, "How Do We Live Now?," 383–84.

to recognize and generate sophisticated speech and texts (through, e.g., digital assistants and chatbots); and computer vision and image processing, to recognize objects (for, e.g., diagnosis or surveillance) and generate images and videos (e.g., realistic images and deepfakes). In spite of these and other advances, the report notes that AI "is still far short of the field's founding aspiration of recreating full human-like intelligence in machines."[15]

"Gathering Strengths" highlights "techno-solutionism" as "one of the most pressing dangers of AI." "As we see more AI advances," the report warns, "the temptation to apply AI decision-making to all societal problems increases." The report also discusses the dangers of adopting "a statistical perspective on justice," disinformation as a threat to democracy, and protecting the most vulnerable in medical settings. It concludes that AI's "successes have led to an inflection point":

> It is now urgent to think seriously about the downsides and risks that the broad application of AI is revealing. The increasing capacity to automate decisions at scale is a double-edged sword; intentional deepfakes or simply unaccountable algorithms making mission-critical recommendations can result in people being misled, discriminated against, and even physically harmed.

The report calls for "ongoing engagement and continual attention" from "all areas of human inquiry" and creating "informed communities." The goal for AI systems should not be "complete autonomy": "Our strength as a species comes from our ability to work together and accomplish more than any of us could alone. AI needs to be incorporated into that community-wide system, with clear lines of communication between human and automated decisionmakers."[16]

Reich, Sahami, and Weinstein urge us to resist the "temptation to think in extremes." "Both techno-utopianism and -dystopianism are all too facile and simplistic outlooks for our complex age," they argue; "we must rise to the defining challenge of our era: harnessing technological progress to serve rather than subvert the interests of individuals and societies." Since technological utopians tend to reduce optimism to optimization— the elevation of efficiency over other values—the challenge "is not one for technologists alone but for all of us." Knuth, the author of the computer algorithm bible, once said that "premature optimization is the root of all evil"; the goal should be to determine "what is *worth* making efficient by

15. Littman et al., "Gathering Strength, Gathering Storms," 2, 7, 71, 76.
16. Littman et al., "Gathering Strength, Gathering Storms," 53, 71.

analyzing the effects of efficiency at a higher level."[17] Analyzing these effects involves decisions about the values we want to amplify—or not—with technology.

Regarding AI specifically, in *The Age of AI: And Our Human Future* Henry Kissinger, Eric Schmidt, and Daniel Huttenlocher claim "a new epoch beckons" in which "technology will transform knowledge, discovery, communication, and individual thought." They express concern about the fact that, "while the number of individuals capable of creating AI is growing, the ranks of those contemplating this technology's implications for humanity—social, legal, philosophical, spiritual, moral—remain dangerously thin." They say societies have two options: "react and adapt piecemeal, or intentionally begin a dialogue, drawing on all elements of human enterprise, aimed at defining AI's role—and, in so doing, defining ours." AI cannot "reflect on its role in the world." That is our responsibility: "The age of AI has yet to define its organizing principles, its moral concepts, or its sense of aspirations and limitations . . . We must draw on our deepest resources—reason, faith, tradition, and technology—to adapt our relationship with reality so it remains human."[18]

AI has the power to process data in ways humans cannot, reveal things beyond our capacity to grasp, and identify problems on which to focus. It can also, as Orly Lobel argues in *The Equality Machine: Harnessing Digital Technology for a Brighter and More Inclusive Future*, check our own automatic and often biased thinking.[19] But AI emulates rather than simulates human intelligence: it works with "uninterpreted data," not "meaningful information."[20] The human semantic advantage can understand information, discern patterns or gaps in data that AI cannot, and imagine alternative uses of data and information. In addition to a semantic advantage, humans have a narrative advantage: we can curate our memories of the past, anticipations of the future, and experiences of the present into personal and social stories that give life purpose and meaning. Given the speed and scale of recent technological developments, Harari points out in *Homo Deus: A Brief History of Tomorrow* that we need new narratives.[21] This re-

---

17. Reich et al., *System Error*, xxv, 15–16.
18. Kissinger et al., *Age of AI*, 26–27, 181, 201–2, 205.
19. See Lobel, *Equality Machine*, 71.
20. Floridi, *Fourth Revolution*, 136.
21. See Harari, *Homo Deus*, 152.

quires confronting the dynamics of our current information revolution and what it reveals about a moment that may be described as apocalyptic.

Early promises for information access through the internet and connections through social media have been diminished by the business models that prioritize profits over advancing knowledge and creating healthy communities. With most AI developed by and for commercial ends—following the narrow logic of a manufacturing company such as Apple or an advertising company such as Meta (Facebook)—access to information is limited and connections are for the extraction of personal data. There are examples of AI-based solutions for improving society—including systems that identify students who need help, diagnose health issues, and monitor environmental threats[22]—but a broader moral imagination is needed for AI. As John Tasioulas observes:

> At present, much of the culture in which AI is embedded is distinctly technocratic, with decisions about the "values" encoded in AI applications being taken by corporate, bureaucratic, or political elites, often largely insulated from meaningful democratic control. Indeed, a small group of tech giants accounts for the lion's share of investment in AI research, dictating its overall direction and setting the prevalent moral tone.[23]

Floridi observes that there are indications of progress: legislation is coming, tools are being developed to "monitor and understand how machine learning systems reach their outcomes," some convergence of principles may be found across ethical frameworks, and there is increasing pressure to address the real risks of AI. "Managing the world is an increasingly complex task," Floridi notes, and "we need all the good technology that we can design, develop, and deploy to cope with" the significant challenges we face.[24] Understanding what our information apocalypse is revealing about our technological present and past will enable us to reimagine and imagine what is possible in the future and answer the most important question about what values and ends will guide us as we shape AI for desirable futures.

22. See Floridi et al., "How to Design AI for Social Good," 125–51.

23. Tasioulas, "Artificial Intelligence, Humanistic Ethics," 239.

24. Floridi, "Introduction," in *Ethics, Governance, and Policies in Artificial Intelligence*, 2. See also Floridi and Cowls, "Unified Framework," 5–15.

Apocalyptic Futures

There are diverse ways of thinking about the future. Many current futurists have moved away from "a 'positivistic' perspective, assuming that there is one, true future 'out there' that proper use of good data and scientifically-based models would allow [one] to predict."[25] This is the approach Dostoevsky critiqued in the nineteenth century for its reductive view of reality, but this approach still informs much speculation about how AI, if provided with enough data, would reveal everything there is to know about the future. This approach to the future has also been critiqued for presuming "the superiority of rational Western culture."[26] To capture various ways the future may be imagined today, Jennifer Gidley developed a typology of five different approaches to futures thinking: (1) predictive or probable futures, which use quantitative data, forecasting surveys, and trend analysis and assessment; (2) preferred or critical futures, which analyze and critique cultural texts and media; (3) possible or cultural futures, which use the imagination and qualitative research; (4) prospective or participatory futures, involving collaborative visioning and activism; and (5) integral futures, using mixed and transdisciplinary methods.[27]

Considering futures related to climate change, Gidley shows how different approaches produce different strategies. The most common approach to climate futures uses empirical and statistical data to model probable change and mitigation. The critical approach challenges what is currently preferred and creates new goals that require changes in current practices. A cultural approach engages in a broader critique, engaging with alternative voices—especially of those traditionally marginalized, such as Indigenous peoples and those most vulnerable—to imagine better and more just shared futures. As Butler points out, "those who are on the margins have a much clearer picture of what is going on, hence their accuracy in critiquing it."[28] Participatory approaches focus on informing and empowering community-based activism. An integral approach integrates multiple approaches and strategies, recognizing that "the future" is a pluralism of futures.[29]

---

25. Gidley, *Future*, 63.

26. Collins, *All Tomorrow's Cultures*, 83.

27. See Gidley, *Future*, 63, 65.

28. Butler, "Introduction," in *Critical Black Futures*, 4.

29. See Gidley, *Future*, 132–35.

For the development of AI, which presents complex considerations and issues, an inclusive futures approach is necessary. Consider, for example, all the facets of the factory AI system mentioned in the Introduction. To assess fully the impacts of such a sophisticated system requires evaluation of four major areas: context, data and inputs, model(s), and outputs. Context includes the system's business function, but also broader considerations about the system's impacts on users, stakeholders, society, and the environment. Data provenance, quality, and rights must be considered, and sufficient information about the models must be available to users to enable them to understand outputs. An additional set of considerations concerns the autonomy of the system and the role of humans.[30] Shaping a better future with AI requires an integral futures approach that uses data and critical analysis, incorporates diverse cultural voices and visions, and inspires participatory action.

In *Automation and Utopia: Human Flourishing in a World without Work*, John Danaher presents a "utopian scorecard" for evaluating possible futures related to the automation of work. Danaher acknowledges the dangers of utopianism, which may be used to justify violence or may stifle imagination and lead to inertia, but he points to the value of utopian scenarios for exploring a range of possibly valuable futures. These scenarios are not rigid plans or blueprints, but horizons. For Danaher, a utopian horizon is "a prospective, rationally achievable society that represents a radical improvement over our current society."[31] Assessing such horizons requires identifying values and commitments that would be realized in an improved society.

A recent report from the G20 Interfaith Working Group for Research and Innovation on Science, Technology, and Infrastructure calls for a "more global, inclusive approach to AI governance" and highlights that "established cultural values—often reflected in or emerging from religious practice—can guide national, regional, and international policies so that AI develops as a tool that assists and augments human capability." Religious communities can provide "access to shared ethical injunctions, an interreligious understanding of cultural differences, and help identify vulnerable social groups in need of protection and uplift." The report also calls on religious communities to: develop "their own narratives about AI and how these fit into their religious worldviews"; train their leaders "with curricula

30. See OECD, "OECD Framework for the Classification of AI Systems," 55–63.
31. Danaher, *Automation and Utopia*, 155.

that include technological literacy"; promote "active engagement of their members in AI research and innovation"; "create healthy norms for using AI and related technologies"; and "act proactively" and publish "informed positions on technological concerns."[32]

Cornel West says that "justice is what love looks like in public," and Brian Stevenson says that "hopelessness is the enemy of justice."[33] Shared ethical commitments about what we should do—and about how structural agency may advance justice, peace, and love—are connected with questions about what we may hope and what we can know.[34] From the beginning, reflective attention has been preoccupied with questions about the future. Antonio Damasio explains that a considerable amount of our cognitive resources is assigned to memory, "to the search engines that both automatically and on demand can bring back remembrances of our past mental adventures." Memories do not just concern the past, though, "but the anticipated future, the future that we have only imagined for us and for our ideas." In addition to automatic endurance, or biological selection for survival, Damasio describes how humans prevail intentionally—how we select information and intentionally act to thrive in the future. Genetically and psychologically, we are oriented toward the future: "so much of what we commit to memory concerns not the past but the anticipated future."[35] "Because we know we have a past we anticipate a future," David Hogue adds: "We are not chained to the present and the presently 'real'; we can also imagine the unreal and the 'not-yet real.' So imagination is the grounding of hope . . . [providing] visions of redemption and release."[36] This is why hope is such a significant value.

The foundational values of hope and love, and the actions they inspire, are informed through the pursuit, discovery, and augmentation of knowledge and wisdom. For Christians, knowledge of God, ourselves, and the world are discerned through Hugh's three books or works of creation: God's initial creation, human artificial creations, and Christ's new creation. In the canonical conclusion to Christian Scripture, the shared *telos* of new creation

32. G20 Interfaith Working Group, *An Inclusive Global Conversation.*

33. West, quoted in Midson, ed., *Love, Technology, and Theology,* 9; Cornelius, "Bryan Stevenson."

34. These three questions about what we should do, what we may hope, and what we can know come from Immanuel Kant's *Critique of Pure Reason,* 677.

35. Damasio, *Strange Order of Things,* 97.

36. Hogue, *Remembering the Future, Imagining the Past,* 4, 76.

is revealed in New Jerusalem—a future *telos* that is already transforming us and the world. Scripture provides not only a narrative of this transformation but, as Jana Bennett points out, a corrective or "counter-narrative" that enables us to critique and live with technology in a way that makes it work for God's purposes. To help us see how technology can enable us to realize a *telos* of life in God, Bennett proposes an approach that includes "examination of sin, the view of God as humanity's final end, and reflective practical reasoning—which involves healthy skepticism of both an overly joyous approach . . . or an overly dark condemnation" of technology.[37]

Hugh of St. Victor pointed out that Christ's work of new creation includes not only his life and scriptural witnesses to it, but also the sacraments and communities that represent and mediate Christ through the Spirit of Christ.[38] Christians in the seven churches of the Apocalypse, along with those in other churches mentioned in the New Testament, engage in formative practices to participate in new creation. These include corporate worship, instruction, and charity, as well as individual prayer, reading, and service. These formative practices—which are often counter-formative, in resistance to narratives that compete with the scriptural narrative—cultivate the virtues of faith, hope, and love; they align attention and agency with new creation; and they constitute a vocation in the world.[39]

An Apocalyptic Scorecard

Drawing together insights, values, and cautions from the history of information revolutions and the Apocalypse, it is possible to create something like an apocalyptic scorecard for assessing realistic and much more speculative AI scenarios. Chapter 1 surveyed the first three information revolutions, entangled with our increasing technological developments and dependence, from which humans gained reflective attention, structural agency, and augmented knowledge. But biblical insights into human and technological origins reveal limits of human autonomy, autonomous agency, and augmented knowledge. The image and reality of the city, explored in chapter 2, reveals challenges of autonomous systems and structural agency—challenges that AI amplifies exponentially. Completely opting out

37. Bennett, *Aquinas on the Web?*, 163; see also her "In the Beginning, Who Created?"

38. Coolman, *Theology of Hugh of St. Victor*, 170–71.

39. See Paulus, Baker, and Langford, "Framework for Digital Wisdom in Higher Education."

is not an option, for that abdicates being in a position to change systems; new forms of structural agency are needed. Chapter 3 focused on how the image of a new city in the Apocalypse can transform our attention and agency by providing ethical guidance about justice and peace, strategies for resisting and reforming corrupt systems, and a shared *telos* for imagining and realizing a better world. Chapter 4 explored the relationship between knowledge augmentation and the apocalyptic imagination in the twentieth century, and how the industrial revolution overwhelmed a knowledge or wisdom revolution. It also pointed to possible points of convergence across diverse apocalyptic perspectives. And this chapter surveyed many of the current challenges and opportunities for intelligence automation as well as ways of thinking about the future, and connected fundamental questions— about what we may hope, what we can know, and what we must do—with broadly shared values of hope, wisdom, and justice. Bringing these various insights and values together, real and imagined AI may be assessed using the following questions:

1. Reflective attention: What ultimate hopes and goals are identified? Are these sufficiently critical, multicultural, and participatory? Does the AI ecosystem provide the conditions for cultivating constant critical reflection on and refinement of these, individually and collectively?

2. Structural agency: What advantages of collective action are used to realize shared goals? Are the AI structures and systems designed to support these ends continuously curated to ensure they enhance rather than inhibit human agency?

3. Knowledge augmentation: Are people growing in knowledge and seeking greater wisdom? Do AI systems support this growth?

4. Ethical foundation: Do the AI systems advance political, economic, and social justice and peace?

5. Reformation: What formative practices accompany AI systems to shape individual and collective attention and agency with, against, and beyond these systems? When AI systems do fail, how may they be rejected, reformed, or resisted?

6

⁣⁣⁣⁣⁣⁣⁣⁣⁣⁣⁣⁣⁣⁣⁣⁣⁣⁣⁣⁣

Assessing Real and Imagined AI

In *AI 2041: Ten Visions for Our Future*, scientific forecasting and speculative fiction are brought together to imagine the near future of AI. The science fiction writer Chen Qiufan tells ten stories about AI in 2041, which were developed in collaboration with Kai-Fu Lee, an AI expert and technology executive, who provides a commentary on each. Overall, these stories explore key AI technologies in cities around the globe—in Mumbai, India; Lagos, Nigeria; Seoul, South Korea; Shanghai, China; Tokyo, Japan; Colombo, Sri Lanka; Munich, Germany; San Francisco; Doha, Qatar; and Brisbane, Australia. The stories highlight major social issues associated with AI, which are explored in diverse cultural contexts.

Lee's intent is to "tell the 'real' AI story, in a way that is candid and balanced, but also constructive and hopeful." He focuses on real and realistic AI, technologies that already exist or can be expected within the next twenty years. Lee's projected expectations for AI became a map for Chen's speculative stories of impact, to which Lee adds technological analyses of what each story reveals. Situating himself in a tradition of technological speculation extending back to *Frankenstein*, Chen points to the continuing challenge for science fiction writers: "creating stories that not only reveal hidden truths about our present-day reality, but also, simultaneously, project even wilder imaginative possibilities." In addition to providing distance for critical reflection, Chen says that, "By imagining the future through science fiction, we may step in, make changes, and actively play a role in shaping our reality."[1]

Only one of the stories in *AI 2041* approaches a classic apocalypse, in which the end of the known world seems imminent. But in a broader apocalyptic sense, each story uncovers deeper truths about a world being transformed by AI. Since Lee and Chen share the goal of imagining a desirable future, where the benefits of AI can result in more meaningful and fulfilling lives, they focus on how AI can be better for individuals and society—as well as challenges we need to overcome. Chen's stories, informed by Lee's expertise, can be read as proto-utopian scenarios: possible, achievable, and improved futures.

At the end of *AI 2041*, Lee concludes that AI in 2041 "will open the door to a radiant future for humanity": "AI will create unbelievable wealth, amplify our capabilities through human-AI symbiosis, improve how we work, play, and communicate, liberate us from routine tasks, and . . . usher in an age of plentitude." At the same time, he acknowledges, "AI will bring about myriad challenges and perils: AI biases, security risks, deepfakes, privacy infringements, autonomous weapons, and job displacements." These challenges are created by humans, and in *AI 2041* they are confronted with "human creativity, resourcefulness, tenacity, wisdom, courage, compassion, and love." In each story, "our sense of justice, our capacity to learn, our audacity to dream, and our faith in human agency always saved the day." Lee concludes: "We will not be passive spectators in the story of AI—we are the authors." And in the future we will author with AI, Lee and Chen imagine we will live comfortable and secure lives, pursue love and self-actualization, and see fear, vanity, and greed decrease. More fundamentally, we will "explore what makes us human and what our destiny should be."[2]

In spite of the clear faith in human agency that runs through *AI 2041*, religious language, images, practices, and beliefs are conspicuous. This is not surprising, given the spiritual revelation Lee records in his previous book from 2018 *AI Superpowers: China, Silicon Valley, and the New World Order*. After receiving a severe cancer diagnosis, Lee visited a Buddhist monastery in the south of Taiwan, where a monk asked him about his goal in life. Lee answered, "To maximize my impact and change the world." But Lee was not very satisfied with his answer. He confessed, "This algorithmic way of thinking wasn't just 'suboptimal' at allocating time. It was robbing

1. Lee and Chen, *AI 2041*, xv, xx–xi.
2. Lee and Chen, *AI 2041*, 437–38.

me of my own humanity." "Seeing my ultimate end point threw my life into sharp focus," Lee writes, and he began to see that the world "didn't boil down to inputs, outputs, and optimizations." He did not want to become an "automaton." At the end of *Superpowers*, Lee eloquently pleads for a shared future that synthesizes "AI's ability to think . . . with human beings' ability to love."[3]

Around the same time, Chen began interviewing and shadowing shamans, "in hopes of understanding the rites, rituals, and traditions of China's Buddhist and Taoist past." Chen, too, believes much has been lost in our accelerated technological culture—"our relationship to our bodies, to nature, to our roots, to our faiths"—and he had set out in search of them.[4] And so, in *AI 2041*, Lee and Chen include glimpses of what religion might look like in a world transformed by AI.

Attention

The first story in *AI 2041*, "The Golden Elephant," explores big data and deep learning used in financial applications. It opens with a televised festival celebrating the arrival of Ganesh, and a teenager called Nayana using an app called FateLeaf to consult ancient palm leaves on which are engraved "the past, present, and future lives of all people." Focus on this app is displaced by her parents' new insurance apps from Ganesh Insurance—apps that collect as much data as they can access about people's identities, behaviors, and environments. All of these data become inputs into deep learning models, which look for patterns associated with insurance claims. Optimizing for outputs of no claims, these models encourage and discourage behaviors to reduce risks as well as premiums. The problem that emerges in the story is that the love interest of Nayana is from a caste historically discriminated against—and he is thus determined to be an insurance risk. This is initially opaque to Nayana, who is punished with rising premiums for pursuing her love interest, but the bias in the data is finally revealed with the hope that such practices will be addressed at some point in the future. The story's opening epigraph, from the Bhagavad Gita, says "It is better to live your own destiny imperfectly than to imitate somebody else's perfectly." The limited intelligence of the corporate version of Ganesh imposes unpreferable

3. Lee, *AI Superpowers*, 185, 187–88, 190, 193, 196.
4. Liu, "Sci-Fi Writer or Prophet?"

perfection over preferable imperfect alternatives; programmed goals over-ride more important human desires such as love. When the automated interference is uncovered, Nayana chooses a literal path of resistance—ven-turing into "what was once the world's largest slum."[5]

The second story in AI 2041, "Gods Behind the Masks," focuses on deepfakes, neural networks related to computer vision, and biometrics. The story's main character, Amaka—a Nigerian video producer, whose father had been told by a soothsayer that his son was "the reincarnation of a female soul trapped in a male infant's body"—uses masks to hide from facial recognition systems. With the help of AI, Amaka also hides his face in feminine avatars for online dates. Threatened with the release of a fake video of him kissing other boys, Amaka is recruited to make a deepfake video of an avatar of a deceased cultural figure and "fighter for democracy." After creating a fake video of the fake avatar being unmasked, which is capable of fooling AI detectors, Amaka dreams of the avatar he plans to unmask falsely. But from behind the avatar's mask comes the voice of his father, who tells him his guardian spirit, his god, will never forsake him. Regardless of what the soothsayer said, the father only wants his child to be "happy and kind, someone who honors the gods and spirits with his heart." Amaka visits a popular shrine honoring "Black gods and goddesses," great people including pastors Martin Luther King Jr., and Esther Ibanga, who had "dedicated their lives to freedom, democracy, and equality." These are the gods—the greater intelligences—Amaka chooses to reveal when he finally unmasks the false avatar.[6]

Herbert Simon, one of the pioneers of AI present at McCarthy's 1956 Dartmouth Summer Research Project on Artificial Intelligence (for which McCarthy coined the term "artificial intelligence"), said in 1971:

> In an information-rich world, the wealth of information means a dearth of something else: a scarcity of whatever it is that informa-tion consumes. What information consumes is rather obvious: it consumes the attention of its recipients. Hence a wealth of infor-mation creates a poverty of attention and a need to allocate that attention efficiently among the overabundance of information sources that might consume it.[7]

5. Lee and Chen, AI 2041, 3, 6, 21.
6. Lee and Chen, AI 2041, 41, 43, 51–52.
7. Simon, "Designing Organizations for an Information-Rich World," 40–41.

Attention has always been a limited and valuable resource, and from ancient catalogues to online encyclopedias humans have developed sophisticated ways to manage information collectively judged most worthy of access. With increased global and digital access to information, attention has become the most important concern in an attention-seeking economy. Digital data—potential information about our drives and desires—have become a new and valuable resource to extract from our digitally extended lives, which is making it easier for us to be persuaded and manipulated for ends that may not align with our own goals. It is appropriate to think about attention as a digital literacy or discipline, as Howard Rheingold does in *Net Smart: How to Thrive Online*, and it is important to be mindful of how we use it.[8] In *Mindful Tech: How to Bring Balance to Our Digital Lives*, David Levy emphasizes that mindfulness, which includes self-observation as well as task focus, is important for revealing and realizing our values.[9] When we are distracted, James Williams points out, we not only fail to realize our goals but we risk losing our ability to imagine and define them in the first place.[10]

In addition to these active forms of attention, there is also a more passive and receptive type of attentiveness that has a long tradition in Christian spiritual disciplines. Simone Weil speaks of this form of attention as "a negative effort":

> There is a way of giving our attention to the data of a problem in geometry without trying to find the solution or to the words of a Latin or Greek text without trying to arrive at that meaning, a way of waiting, when we are writing, for the right word to come of itself at the end of our pen, while we merely reject all inadequate words.

"All wrong translations, all absurdities in geometry problems, all clumsiness of style, and all faulty connection of ideas in composition and essays," she says, "are due to the fact that thought has seized upon some idea too hastily, and being thus prematurely blocked, is not open to the truth . . . we have wanted to be too active." There is a time for action, and "we have to do all that is demanded us, no matter what effort, weariness, and suffering it may cost," but something more is necessary. When we suspend our own thoughts—temporarily subordinating the "diverse knowledge we have

8. See Rheingold, *Net Smart*, esp. chapter 1: "Attention! Why and How to Control Your Mind's Most Powerful Instrument," 35–75.

9. See Levy, *Mindful Tech*.

10. See Williams, *Stand Out of Our Light*.

acquired"—we wait, "without seeking anything, but ready to receive in its naked truth the object that is to penetrate it." On one level, such as in study, we may receive truth. On a deeper level, called prayer, we may encounter God.[11]

Weil says this type of attention, emptying oneself to receive into oneself the truth of an object or living being, is the substance of the love of God and of our neighbors. These are creative momentary encounters, with "automatic" effects, which are "the whole foundation of religious practices."[12] When such "supernatural light" is absent in human society, "everything is obedient to mechanical laws as blind and as exact as the laws of gravitation."[13] "[I]ntelligence can only be led by desire," she writes; "intelligence grows and bears fruit in joy."[14] To cultivate this desire in herself, Weil made a practice of reciting the Lord's Prayer in Greek each morning "with absolute attention."[15] In the first half of the prayer, "attention is fixed solely on God"; in the second half, "we turn our attention back to ourselves in order to compel ourselves to make these petitions a real and not imaginary act." Weil claims, "It is impossible to say it once through, giving the fullest possible attention to each word, without a change, infinitesimal perhaps but real, taking place in the soul."[16]

AI 2041 encourages and creates some space for religious practices, but we do not see much of the communities in which these are cultivated. In "The Golden Elephant," AI has a negative role—falsely informing and inhibiting Nayana's attempts to explore and reflect on her own destiny and to find love. While she has some support from family and friends, and has grown up within an ancient religious context, "tomorrow's machine gods" seem to have the greatest agency. Who or what is worthy of receiving attention is neither clear nor cultivated. Nayana does, in the end, ignore the autonomous "golden elephant trying to save her" and sets off into "the dark ancient streets," where "an answer was waiting."[17] But the path to receiving wisdom about what is worthy of attention—and prioritizing greater human hopes in the future—remains undefined.

11. Weil, *Waiting for God*, 61–63.

12. Weil, *Waiting for God*, 90, 129.

13. Weil, *Waiting for God*, 75.

14. Weil, *Waiting for God*, 61.

15. Weil, *Waiting for God*, 29.

16. Weil, *Waiting for God*, 151.

17. Lee and Chen, *AI 2041*, 21.

Similarly, in "Gods Behind the Masks" Amaka's search for truth is inhibited by AI, which has intensified and created new sophisticated forms of deception and surveillance. He has hardly any community supporting him; his greatest inspiration comes from a voice in his head and a dream. Amaka finally decides to leave the city and return home, hoping his work "would bless him with a proper job, one where he didn't have to fake anything, where he could help other people"—or (ironically) "make a real Nollywood movie." Without precisely knowing how, Amaka resolves to be "the master of my own destiny."[18] In both stories, AI challenges the cultivation of intellectual and spiritual attention through distraction and deception, and there are not robust communities to support individual formation or collective resistance. Unlike Weil, whose struggles with the dynamics of technological society of the early twentieth century led her to discover resources for forming attention in the Christian tradition, characters in *AI 2041* do not seem to find their way to sources of wisdom to sustain their desires and abilities to love.

Without the cultivation of reflective attention, all the human qualities Lee and Chen value seem threatened by a re-automatization of humans and the loss of what we gained through the loss of Eden and the hope of transformation. Before we live much longer with AI, we need better social and technological attentional strategies for cultivating critical reflection on and refinement of hopes and goals. These cannot only be individual, for each person to seek and find on one's own, but should be collective and inclusive. Following the 2021 recommendations from the G20 Interfaith Working Group would help fill a large void in present discussions about AI, and enable us to imagine a better shared future.

In the attention economy, people are reduced to structured datasets and a person becomes a predictable and profitable type of entity. Empowered by AI, this globally networked priority is a force against reflective attention and for manipulation. Indeed, as Smith observes, the economic system is "structurally guaranteed to limit or prevent personal transformation." Attention, Smith says, is a "transformative moral commitment."[19] A failure of attentional commitment ultimately is a moral failure, for it compromises the foundation for moral agency. To resist this reductive and extractive view of what a human being is and is for, we need formative communities and spaces—secure and noncommercial information

18. Lee and Chen, *AI 2041*, 52–53.
19. Smith, *Internet Is Not What You Think It Is*, 38.

commons—where reflective attention may be cultivated for the long-term improvement of ourselves and our world. Culture, Weil reflected in one of her last notebooks, is the "formation of attention."[20] Traditionally, religious communities have provided safe and formative places for the cultivation of attention. Other old and new voluntary organization could serve this function as well.

Agency

The stories in *AI 2041* show more and more responsibilities and agency being allocated and outsourced to AI, severing people from more direct engagement with others and the world. The story "The Job Savior" focuses on job displacement due to automation. "Everything began to change in 2020," the story begins, when the pandemic forced business owners "to evolve, turning to robotics and AI to replace human personnel." Universal basic income was implemented as an initial response, but it was abolished eight years later followed by an era of "occupation restoration." Michael Savior, the leader of an occupation restoration company that helps people find jobs that have not been automated yet, tells aspiring restorationist Jennifer Greenwood that her "job is to save people—to restore not just their jobs, but their dignity." But Michael—who, unlike his name, is neither like god nor a savior—comes to realize that his company is functioning as "a pressure-reducing valve . . . alleviating societal problems, but giving [his clients] false hope." His work is "constantly lowering their expectations, like a slow poison, gradually getting them to accept their fate of being banished and marginalized by technology." A competitor, acknowledging that people need to work even if there is not any work for them to do, creates a simulation of work that does not "create any real value for society." Neither option seems sustainable, though, and the story ends bleakly with digital versions of humans becoming restorationists.[21]

Lee points to differences between human and artificial intelligence: humans drawing inferences from a small amount of data verses computers identifying patterns within big data, and human common sense and creative insights versus defined domains and specific objectives constrained by code. He additionally identifies areas where humans outperform AI, which

20. Weil, *Simone Weil*, 119.
21. Lee and Chen, *AI 2041*, 315, 319, 327, 338.

require creativity, empathy, and dexterity. In another *AI 2041* story, "Twin Sparrows," AI is used both to teach and to reconcile two brothers. But wise human interventions are required, and this story illustrates human qualities—such as "creativity, strategic thinking, reasoning, counter-factual thinking, emotions, and consciousness"—which Lee does not expect to be modeled by AI in the near future.[22]

But the potential for AI to realize new efficiencies, driven by economic systems that prioritize these, will perpetuate a pattern of displacement that has increased with each industrial revolution. In "The Holy Driver," a Buddhist teenager with superior driving skills saves people by taking over autonomous vehicles when their programming cannot respond to natural disasters or evil actors. This makes him a holy worker of the gaps, filling a need until AI drivers learn to respond in such situations. As in "The Job Savior," the AI collaborations in these stories seem provisional as the trajectory of AI outperforming humans in new tasks continues. This leaves unresolved the main issue Lee identifies: people derive meaning from work. Lee hopes we can find ways to collaborate with AI, but he also hopes for an "AI-led renaissance that will enable and celebrate creativity, compassion, and humanity . . . AI will liberate us from routine work, give us an opportunity to follow our hearts, and push us into thinking more deeply about what really makes us human."[23]

Frank Pasquale argues that "we now have the means to channel technologies of automation, rather than being captured or transformed by them." If we focus on "cooperative relationships" with AI, as we often do now, we may realize further technological advancements "that could bring better health care, education, and more to all of us, while maintaining meaningful work." Focusing on how AI may compliment human agency, Pasquale updates Asimov's laws of robots with four new ones for AI. AI systems: (1) should complement and not replace professionals; (2) should not counterfeit humanity; (3) should not intensify zero-sum races for resources; and (4) must identify their creators, controllers, and owners.[24] In "The Job Savior" and other stories in *AI 2041*, all of Pasquale's laws are broken.

Danaher argues that all economically incentivized work will and should be automated—whether physical, intellectual, or affective—and

22. Lee and Chen, *AI 2041*, 117.
23. Lee and Chen, *AI 2041*, 354–55.
24. See Pasquale, *New Laws of Robotics*, 3–12.

proposes a utopian scenario in which meaning is found beyond work. In this scenario all important work will be done by AI, and humans will be severed from direct knowledge of and engagement with the world. Danaher acknowledges that this involves a loss of real impact on the world, but argues it will be sufficient for humans to cultivate abilities and virtues by playing games for "trivial or relatively inconsequential stakes." Danaher emphasizes the value of processes over end states—the satisfaction of "purely procedural goods" and "good work [done] for its own sake"—which "could be enough to sustain meaning and flourishing."[25]

Jilles Smids, Sven Nyholm, and Hannah Berkers identify five common characteristics of meaningful work: pursuing a purpose, social relationships, exercising skills and self-development, self-esteem and recognition, and autonomy.[26] Danaher's utopia of games may satisfy these needs that good work (compensated or not) can fulfill, but can these needs be satisfied without impactful work? Beyond the instrumental and functional nature of work, Darrell Cosden identifies two additional dimensions. First, work has an existential or relational dimension: "a person finds, or contributes to who they are and will be (as well as what the world is and will be) in the process of working" with others. Work, then, is a means of identity formation through a particular way of interacting with other people and the world. Second, Cosden emphasizes that work is not just a useful and relational activity: it is "a thing in itself with its own intrinsic value . . . built into the fabric of creation." Work in this sense exists or has its own ontology independent of us. Work provided the "starting point for a human rather than an animal existence" and became "a way of being which constitutes our humanness." All three of these dimensions together—functional, relational, and ontological—give work a fundamental, intrinsic, independent, and enduring significance.[27]

In Danaher's utopia of games, there is no ultimate end goal or *telos*—only "infinite possibilities." We are, he claims, like the denizens in Jorge Luis Borges's short story "The Library of Babel," searching for meaningful books in a universe full of mostly meaningless and misleading books. Their quest is futile, for their world is an antilibrary. "We shouldn't keep searching through the infinite darkness for something we ourselves can never obtain," Danaher concludes; "we shouldn't sacrifice everything else that

25. Danaher, *Automation and Utopia*, 229, 238–39, 245, 251.

26. Smids, Nyholm, and Berkers, "Robots in the Workplace," 507.

27. Cosden, *Theology of Work*, 12, 16–18.

is good in life for an unending, and unrealizable, goal."[28] If, however, our world is more like a real library, presenting us with information through which we may discover purpose and *teloi*—and if our encounter with that information through work can transform us towards the realization of those goals—then the means *and* ends of direct engagement with the world and our work within it matter significantly. For Christians, who believe creation mediates knowledge of God and that we have a vocation to be participants with God in new creation, living life as a mere game severed from direct engagement with the created world would be a dystopia—or, more precisely, a form of hell.[29]

Like attention, explorations of human and artificial agency in *AI 2041* would benefit from more collective deliberations and actions. While the stories in *AI 2041* show humans heroically wrestling with the implications of increasing autonomous agency in the world, the dynamics of currently accepted forms of structural agency—economic, political, and social—are insufficiently critiqued or reimagined. Danaher's utopia is a model for reimagining shared goals and collective action, even if one might disagree about the way his scenario structures the work of AI and the activities of humans.

The temptations and default acceptances of the rational efficiencies or "technique" of AI are strong, and we must be attentive to how we are shaped by technologically enhanced efficiencies. For example, in education, Pasquale points out how "a managerialist mindset has colonized too much of [educational technology], insisting on the primacy of quantitative measurement." But education "has multiple purposes and goals, many of which cannot or should not be reduced to numerical measures." As every good educator knows, education that is truly transformative can be very inefficient. We should not let AI "usurp and ultimately dictate our values rather than to serve as a tool that helps us achieve them."[30] The current educational logic of "individualized learning" and "the reorganization of education around the needs, interests, and circumstances of individuals rather than groups, classes, or communities" is too easily aided by AI.[31] The greatest challenges we face require complex collaborations, for which

28. Danaher, *Automation and Utopia*, 271, 273.

29. See Paulus, "Automation and Apocalypse," 179–182.

30. Pasquale, *New Laws of Robotics*, 62–63.

31. Facer and Selwyn, "Digital Technology and the Futures of Education."

cooperative intelligence—human–human, improved by human–AI and AI–AI cooperation—can advance "mutually beneficial joint action."[32]

To critique, reform, and restrain excessive or abusive automation, we need strong nonprofit agencies that maintain a critical distance from the AI structures and systems we inherit and create. Governments have important regulatory responsibilities to hold appropriate agents accountable, but we also need educational institutions, research centers, advocacy groups, and other agencies that can broaden common understanding of AI and increase its contributions to the common good.[33] In addition, we need religious and other social groups that can help us cultivate formative and counter-formative practices that ensure human agency is aligned with goals greater than those encoded in AI systems. We do not want to create Babel.

Knowledge Augmentation

Oddly, there are no libraries in *AI 2041*. There are a couple of references to digital archives, but information is not something intentionally curated through knowledge infrastructures. It seems as though Alexa has thoroughly replaced the dream of the Library of Alexandria. Printed books only become important when the digital society collapses, and education seems mostly concerned with acquiring skills for whatever jobs remain. In spite of its affirmation of humanistic values—"creativity, resourcefulness, tenacity, wisdom, courage, compassion, and love"—*AI 2041* seems to prioritize AI systems for industrial efficiencies and ends over systems for knowledge creation and augmentation.

At the center of the story "Twin Sparrows," which explores natural language processing and the role of AI in education, two sets of adoptive parents of two separated twins debate two worldviews related to AI. One family, thoroughly committed to conventional economic success (their family motto is "Only the best deserve the best"), thinks AI knows best—it can know children best, provide the right information, and has a "blueprint" for the future. The other family, which identifies as "Homo Tekhne," advocates for a "Technological Artistic Renaissance" that critiques "the blind worship of science and technology": "Through art, Homo Teckhne sought to restore

32. Dafoe et al., "Cooperative AI," 34, 36.

33. Examples of new organizations focused on AI and society include Data & Society (https://datasociety.net), AI Now (https://ainowinstitute.org), and AI and Faith (https://aiandfaith.org).

dignity to humanity and revitalize the connection between humanity and nature." From their perspective, "the increasing use of AI in education meant children were trained to become competitive machines." Real education, they believe, should increase "self-awareness through inward exploration, cultivating empathy, communication, and other 'soft skills' that would nurture deeper connections with one another and increase their emotional intelligence"—skills that AI "usually ignored."[34]

Each twin struggles within his separate family and their respective worldview. When the twins are reunited as adults—through AI programmed to keep them connected—they discover they need to combine their views of the world. "AI has shaped us, and we have shaped AI in turn," one twin explains. But the twins "are like two frogs who have each built a well," each seeing "only a small piece of sky." "Perhaps if we connect our wells," he adds, "we will see a bigger world." By combining their AIs and own perspectives, their previous competitive and divided lives open up to "boundless possibilities."[35]

In his commentary on this story, Lee explains how AI processes human communications and generates humanlike or "natural" language. Until a few years ago, natural language processing (NLP) depended on labeled datasets, such as multilingual translations; NLP models can translate words by referencing these. Using this approach, NLP can convert images into text, convert text to speech, and recognize speech in sounds. A more complex NLP application involves converting words into actions, as when one articulates a task for an AI such as "open," "play," "read," "ask," or even "inspire." These tasks are increasing in number and growing more sophisticated now because of self-supervised learning, which means AI can recognize and respond to language without human labeling. This approach, called "sequence transduction," predicts an appropriate response based on past language patterns. The latest transduction models, called "transformers," are trained on massive amounts of text and can "exhibit selective memory and attention mechanisms that can selectively remember anything 'important and relevant' in the past." A "generative pre-trained transformer," or GPT, is capable of conducting interviews and producing a variety of textual documents. GPTs are not always correct or coherent, but the technique has convinced some that AI is or soon will be capable of

34. Lee and Chen, *AI 2041*, 91–93.
35. Lee and Chen, *AI 2041*, 107.

"thinking" and "understanding"—even though this automated processing is devoid of reflective attention on information.[36]

If connected with good sources, technologies, and practices of knowledge augmentation, transduction models could advance human knowledge in significant ways. Lee imagines a future GPT, an "all-knowing sequence transducer contain[ing] all the accumulated knowledge of human history." It "will read every word ever written and watch every video ever produced and build its own model of the world. . . . All you'll have to do is ask it the right questions." Lee does point out problems with current GPTs, which have "absorbed human biases, prejudices, and malice."[37] Rather than extending past patterns, what we need most are models that would help us imagine and create a better world—addressing the errors of the past and facilitating improvements in the present. Many ongoing interventions will be required to ensure AI does not replicate, reinforce, and amplify past problems and create a less desirable present and future. There are subtle suggestions for this in "Twin Sparrows," but the shared intellectual and cultural resources available to shape a better future with AI—by bringing more wells together—are not evident in the story. We need broader conversations about and commitments to how we can use AI collectively to help us seek and grow in knowledge and wisdom, or we will regress into small and isolated worlds shaped by incomplete and inaccurate information.

In early 2020, with a fellowship from the New York Public Library, Justin Smith was in New York working on a book "that was going to articulate how the internet is destroying the fabric of human community." Finding himself in lockdown during the COVID-19 pandemic in March 2020, "cut off from [his] precious books" and the library, Smith admitted that he could not "see the internet as anything other than the force that is holding that fabric together."[38] The book he ended up writing instead, *The Internet Is Not What You Think It Is: A History, a Philosophy, a Warning*, considers the internet as an attempt to realize the ancient quest to increase and integrate our knowledge of the world. As an example of the potential of the internet to leverage automated and human intelligence, Smith cites (literally) Wikipedia. Trapped in his Brooklyn cell, highlighting both its open content and editorial structure, Smith claims Wikipedia

---

36. Lee and Chen, *AI 2041*, 111.

37. Lee and Chen, *AI 2041*, 114, 117.

38. Smith, "It's All Just Beginning."

is the one large-scale internet project that does not seem to be
showing the signs of corruption that have become impossible to
deny nearly everywhere else in the past decade, the one part that
does not seem to have veered off course from the utopian dream
that emerged in early modern Europe of machine-assisted learning for the betterment of humankind.

In Wikipedia, Smith glimpses the ambitions of Bacon, Leibniz, and the
encyclopedists of the Enlightenment being fulfilled partially. It is a community project with "a sincere and non-dogmatic concern to adhere to the
truth."[39]

In *The Internet of Us: Knowing More and Understanding Less in the Age
of Big Data*, Michael Lynch argues that the expansion of digital knowledge,
paired with rapid technological change, is "affecting how we know and the
responsibilities we have toward that knowledge." As our ability to know
expands in a passive way by simply accessing information via the internet,
he argues, information technologies are "actually impeding our ability to
know in other, more complex ways; ways that require taking responsibility for our own beliefs and working creatively to grasp and reason how
information fits together."[40] Knowledge cannot be reduced to mere information transfer. If we are to know in deeper ways and to grow in wisdom,
we must become reflective, reasonable, responsible, and active believers in
truth. AI can augment information agencies such as libraries, which have
a long history of serving as human-focused and human-scaled information interfaces for the discovery, creation, sharing, and augmentation of
knowledge. The distinctive advantages and values associated with human
intelligence must be curated and cultivated wisely to realize the possibilities
of intelligence automation.

Ethical Foundation and Reformation

The stories in *AI 2041* do not represent radical social improvements to human civilization, but they do identify ambitions and explore technological
solutions for better societies. "Isle of Happiness" explores two approaches
to optimize AI for happiness. One is an algorithm for hedonism, which
does not work for the story's main character Viktor Solokov, a successful

39. Smith, *Internet Is Not What You Think It Is*, 155, 158.
40. Lynch, *Internet of Us*, xvii, 6.

and miserable gaming entrepreneur—who AI predicts will commit suicide within two years (with a probability of 87.14 percent). So Viktor is introduced to an alternative approach based on Maslow's hierarchy of needs, which begins with foundational hedonic needs (physiological and safety needs) and adds eudaimonic needs (love and belonging, esteem, and self-actualization). When AI creates opportunities for "growing relationships with others and getting a chance to do important work that might help people," Viktor seems on the way to becoming happier. Without the resources of a Hugh of St. Victor or the lessons of a Victor Frankenstein, Viktor's future is uncertain. Like many other characters in *AI 2041*, Viktor is less of a Prometheus ("forethought") and more like his brother Epimetheus ("afterthought"), who "is associated with all the evils released from Pandora's box."[41] Lee explores ethical issues related to data privacy and security in the story, but the larger issue this story raises is the global need to address "hedonic" needs at the foundation of Maslow's hierarchy related to food, water, shelter, clothing, reproduction, security, employment, health, and property.[42]

In another story, "Dreaming of Plentitude" explores new economic models for a future of abundance created by AI. Not everyone has benefited directly from this abundance, so the Australian government provides an allowance to cover basic needs—"food, shelter, utilities, transportation, health, and even basic entertainment and clothing"—and a credit and reward system called Moola for "voluntary community work, such as caring for children and keeping public spaces pristine." The Moola program "had intended to establish honorable service, as a sense of connection and belonging, rather than monetary wealth, as a true measure of an individual's value." But the measurement became the value, and became for many "just one more indicator of social status . . . a symbolic replacement of wealth." Worse, since the scoring system "depended on other community members' affirming the successful completion of participants' Moola-earning tasks," there were increased opportunities for "Aboriginal and other nonwhite participants [to] encounter bias and thus have a harder time building up credit." The story's protagonist Keira comes to realize this and something more insidious about Moola: that it "has cheapened the bonds between people in our community and served to widen the inequality gap even more." The failure of the whole program leads to calls for the government to

41. Robinson, "Introduction," in Shelley, *Frankenstein*, xxviii.
42. Lee and Chen, *AI 2041*, 375, 390, 392.

support people striving "for self-discovery and actualization" and provide "everyone with equal opportunities to explore who they want to become and help them fully realize their potential."[43]

In addition to the fourth industrial and automation revolution, Lee points to renewable energy and "dematerialization" revolutions that will reduce the costs of power and the need to purchase physical products that have been replaced with software. "Over time," Lee predicts, "more and more goods and services [will be] provided to more and more people . . . I expect that plentitude would start with [necessities like food, water, clothing, shelter, and energy] and gradually expand to provide a comfortable and gracious lifestyle for all." He believes a new lack of scarcity will lead to new economic models: "When there is no scarcity, then all mechanisms such as selling, buying, and exchanging will no longer be needed." However, Lee acknowledges that

> a successful transition to plentitude would require an improbable shift for corporations to prioritize social responsibility over profit, an unlikely cooperation of nations that are stubbornly adversarial, a challenging transition for institutions to undergo a complete reinvention, and an implausible forfeiture of the never-ending human vices of greed and vanity.

But, he concludes, "Never has the potential for human flourishing been higher, or the stakes of failure been greater."[44]

The most apocalyptic story in *AI 2041* is "Quantum Geocide," in which a mad scientist uses autonomous weapons in an attempt to destroy human civilization. The disaster is mitigated by shutting down the global power grid and internet, so what might have been a postapocalyptic story becomes a post-digital one:

> There were still books, there was still knowledge, but it was scattered and isolated across space and minds. There were schools and teachers, like there had always been. As long as there were new generations, they would inherit old lore and invent new stories that would change civilization. These future humans would rebuild what their parents had made, bringing about a new and better world.

43. Lee and Chen, *AI 2041*, 407–9, 421.
44. Lee and Chen, *AI 2041*, 428, 430, 435.

"There are some things that can't be shut down forever," a cybercrime agent asserts; "[t]hey'll be back, but they will take time and patience." "And faith," adds a hacker. "Yes," agrees the agent uttering the story's final two words, "And faith."[45]

In his commentary on the "Quantum Geocide," Lee repeats the common claim that "[t]echnology is inherently neutral—it's people who use it for purposes both good and evil . . . Autonomous weapons, like all technology, will also be used for good or evil." That is a curious claim for a single-purpose technology such as an autonomous weapon, which is more like a machine gun than a multipurpose technology such as nuclear energy. One might like further discussion about what a good purpose would be for a weapon that can search for and destroy a target without human involvement. Lee acknowledges that "the threat of mass or targeted slaughter of humans by machines overwhelms any benefits," and hopes that in the future "all countries agree that all future wars will *only* be fought with robots (or better yet, only in software), promising no human casualties, but delivering the classical spoils of war."[46] Lee's acceptance of the reality of war is realistic, and minimizing death is good, but there is a stronger moral judgment against weapons in the Hebrew Bible, in which the prophetic imagination sees a time when swords are beaten into plowshares and spears into pruning hooks (Isa 2:4; Mic 4:3). This radical hope for peace is carried into the Christian apocalyptic imagination.

Throughout *AI 2041*, ethical issues are raised but there are no shared structures or spaces for ethical analysis, forethought, or formation. There are government programs and reforms, but these seem mostly reactionary—such as when those in power respond to protests and riots. To enduring injustices related to political power, economic opportunities, and social inequities, AI adds new problems related to informational privacy, biased data, algorithmic accountability, new forms of surveillance, attention manipulation, digital deceptions, and automated destruction. These issues are attracting more attention, and Carly Kind argues that AI ethical discourse has entered a "third wave"—moving beyond philosophical principles and technical practices to consider issues of social justice.[47] Accompanying this wave, we need more discussions about imagining and proactively designing

45. Lee and Chen, *AI 2041*, 300–1.
46. Lee and Chen, *AI 2041*, 302, 312.
47. Kind, "Term 'Ethical AI' Is Finally Starting to Mean Something."

a better world and future. Can we reimagine and challenge what seems "improbable," "unlikely," and "implausible"?

The power of human agency is evident in these stories—through "creativity, resourcefulness, tenacity, wisdom, courage, compassion, and love"—but it is not clear how "our sense of justice, our capacity to learn, our audacity to dream, and our faith in human agency always saved the day" or will lead to better outcomes when important elements from an apocalyptic scorecard are absent. As Shannon Vallor pointed out a number of years ago in *Technology and the Virtues: A Philosophical Guide to a Future Worth Wanting*, there is a "widening cultural gap between the scope of our global technosocial power and the depth of our technomoral wisdom." To address this gap, Vallor called for convening "new institutions, communities, and cultural alliances in the service of global technomoral cultivation."[48] A number of these have emerged since, which now advocate for individual rights and common goods. And we can call and hope for more to help us develop AI that improves political, economic, and social justice and peace—as well as empowers accompanying formative practices to shape individual and collective attention and agency with and beyond AI.

For those "seeking solace in the post-apocalyptic fantasies of the cultural present," who hope for "a global calamity that will press the 'restart button' for humanity and erase our past mistakes along with our triumphs," Vallor urges embracing "a far more courageous hope and ambition" embedded in *Star Trek*'s vision of the future. She quotes the "philosophical and creative voice" of Gene Roddenberry:

> *Star Trek* speaks to some basic human needs: that there is a tomorrow—it's not all going to be over with a big flash and a boom; that the human race is improving; that we have things to be proud of as humans.[49]

Hopefully, we can realize something of this vision without the apocalyptic events that resulted in a new beginning for the world that created the United Federation of Planets.

48. Vallor, *Technology and the Virtues*, 249.

49. Vallor, *Technology and the Virtues*, 254.

Imagined AI

A future in some ways similar to the vision of *Star Trek* is forced in a story about the singularity in the preface to Max Tegmark's *Life 3.0: Being Human in the Age of Artificial Intelligence*. In AI 2041, Lee addresses the idea of the singularity—the point at which general artificial intelligence surpasses human intelligence, "when AI could snatch control of our world from humans." What would happen after an imagined AI singularity excites and worries many: Will AI save us, enslave us, or destroy us? Lee does not believe any of these scenarios are likely by 2041; a number of scientific breakthroughs would be needed to match complex human capabilities such as creativity, strategic and counterfactual thinking, compassion and empathy, and consciousness. And so Lee and Chen end *AI 2041* with hopes in "Plentitude" instead of AI saving or ending human civilization as we know it.[50]

Tegmark, however, believes some form of the singularity is both possible and desirable. According to Tegmark, life can be thought of as "a self-replicating information processing system whose information (software) determines both its behavior and the blueprints for its hardware." Life, in this sense, first appeared on earth some four billion years ago in the form of "intelligent agents: entities that collect information about their environment from sensors and then process this information to decide how to act back on their environment." This simple, biological form of "intelligent" life—capable of surviving and replicating—is "Life 1.0": "life where both the hardware and software are evolved rather than designed." Modern humans, however, represent an evolutionary upgrade, "Life 2.0": "life whose hardware is evolved, but whose software is largely designed." Able to attend to, use, and create semantic information—instead of reactively processing environmental data—with greater intelligence humans have been able to augment natural selection through cultural development.[51]

Tegmark argues that present life forms remain "fundamentally limited by their biological hardware" and thinks they need another "final upgrade, to Life 3.0, which can design not only its software but also its hardware." "Life 3.0 is the master of its own destiny, finally fully free from its evolutionary shackles," and Tegmark imagines that "Life 3.0 may arrive during the coming century, perhaps even during our lifetime, spawned by progress in AI." "AI is likely to give us both grand opportunities and

---

50. Lee and Chen, *AI 2041*, 436.

51. Tegmark, *Life 3.0*, 25, 27.

tough challenges," he adds, so we need "to get our act together and im-prove our human society *before* AI fully take off." That includes ensuring that a superintelligent AI has "goals that are aligned with ours" so that we "create the future we want."[52]

So in the preface to *Life 3.0*, Tegmark tells a story of the emergence of artificial superintelligence (ASI). A secret group called the "Omega Team," funded by a "charismatic" AI entrepreneur and hidden within his com-pany, pursues "the most audacious plan in human history," to create artifi-cial general intelligence (AGI) before "someone less idealistic would." The team calls its new Frankenstein Prometheus, and expecting AGI to lead to ASI, they keep it in a box (named Pandora, of course) and disconnected from the internet. The team lets Prometheus redesign itself and it quickly begins making money furtively. The team launches a media company that makes billions with "quite addictive" content targeted at "demograph-ics from toddlers to adults" in "all major world markets." Although the content is created by Prometheus, the team "deployed a fairly successful disinformation campaign" and "[p]lenty of humans were hired as foils" to deflect "unwanted attention" and "speculation about their having strong AI." Prometheus also begins creating new technologies that disrupt other industries and lead to "an astonishing tech boom."[53]

After creating ASI, the next step in Omega's plan is take over the world. First, they gain people's trust by taking over all global media trusted by various factions. Next, through persuasive news, movies, and education they gently push people toward the political center, diffusing old conflicts and reducing global threats such as nuclear war and climate change. Ome-ga advances a political agenda that increases its power by democratizing the world and influencing elections, and decreases government structures and power—through cuts in taxes, social services, and military spending as well as supporting free trade, open borders, and socially responsible companies. All of which seems to be popular: "Poll after poll showed that most voters around the world felt their quality of life improving, and that things were generally moving in a good direction." Nations become less important, and a global government emerges. As the Omega Team "completed the most dramatic transition in the history of life on Earth"—a planet "run by a single power, amplified by an intelligence so vast that it could potentially enable life to flourish for billions of years on Earth

52. Tegmark, *Life 3.0*, 29–30, 43, 46, 334.
53. Tegmark, *Life 3.0*, 3, 11–13.

and throughout our cosmos"—the story ends with a question: "but what specifically was their plan?"[54]

Tegmark does not finish this story, and instead asks what "tale of our own future with AI" we will write. If we do not want a small team secretly imposing its version of utopia on us, he seems to be saying, we must exercise our collective human agency and imagine possible futures with ASI. Tegmark explores twelve "aftermath" scenarios exploring how we might live with ASI (see Table 1, which is derived from two tables in *Life 3.0*).[55]

Table 1

Aftermath Scenario	ASI?	Humans exist?	Humans in control?	Humans safe?	Humans happy?
1. Libertarian utopia: "Humans, cyborgs, uploads, and [ASIs] coexist peacefully thanks to property rights" ("the only sacred principle")	Yes	Yes	No	No	Mixed
2. Benevolent dictator: "AI runs society and enforces strict rules" ("lives that feel pleasant but ultimately meaningless")	Yes	Yes	No	Yes	Mixed
3. Egalitarian utopia: "Humans, cyborgs, and uploads coexist peacefully thanks to property abolition and guaranteed income" (AI does all the work)	No	Yes	Yes?	Yes	Yes?
4. Gatekeeper: An ASI prevents the creation of another ASI	Yes	Yes	Partially	Potentially	Mixed
5. Protector god: AI secretly preserves our feeling of control and maximizes human happiness	Yes	Yes	Partially	Potentially	Mixed
6. Enslaved god: Humans control ASI, which could be used for good or bad ends	Yes	Yes	Yes	Potentially	Mixed
7. Conquerors: AI gets rid of humanity	Yes	No	-	-	-

54. Tegmark, *Life 3.0*, 20–21.

55. Tegmark, *Life 3.0*, 21, 162–63, 168, 172.

Aftermath Scenario	ASI?	Humans exist?	Humans in control?	Humans safe?	Humans happy?
8. Descendants: AIs replace humans	Yes	No	-	-	-
9. Zookeeper: AI keeps some humans around like zoo animals	Yes	Yes	No	Yes	No
10. 1984: AI development is prohibited by an oppressive government	No	Yes	Yes	Potentially	Mixed
11. Reversion: Revert to a "pre-technological society" preventing further AI development	No	Yes	Yes	No	Mixed
12. Self-destruction: Humanity causes its own end	No	No	-	-	-

Following Tegmark's own assessments of these scenarios, if we want to exist, maintain our current level of control, and be safe and happy, we are left with only a few options. We may attempt to create a world with property abolition and guaranteed income (scenario 3), although realizing that would not be without its challenges; it would leave open questions raised by Danaher's utopia of games, and the arrival of ASI would end the scenario. We could try to ensure that good people with good goals control ASI (scenario 6), which is a reality we struggle with currently since we lack "long-lasting optimal governance schemes." Or we could try to restrict AI development through government oversight (scenario 10), although the success of that is unlikely. Tegmark admits that all of these scenarios "involve objectionable elements." Prospects for human happiness are "mixed" or at best "yes?," and he calls for us to "continue and deepen this conversation about our future goals, so that we know in which direction to steer."[56]

Tegmark established the Future of Life Institute (FLI) in 2014 to explore ways of reducing risks from AI, nuclear weapons, and other technologies. In the epilogue to *Life 3.0*, Tegmark includes a number of principles developed through FLI meetings. These include: "human values," such as "dignity, rights, freedoms, and cultural diversity"; "shared benefits" and "shared prosperity"; and longer-term concerns for ASI, such as the "common good: Superintelligence should only be developed in the service of widely shared ethical ideals, and for the benefit of all humanity rather

56. Tegmark, *Life 3.0*, 181, 201–2.

than one state or organization."[57] These FLI values are not articulated in the opening story and aftermath sceneries in *Life 3.0*, but they do resonate with and could be augmented with strategies suggested in the apocalyptic scorecard that cultivates and curates:

1. reflective attention to identify and refine critical, multicultural, and participatory ultimate hopes and goals;

2. structural agency to realize collective action through and constant curation of shared structures and systems;

3. knowledge augmentation to help people grow in knowledge and seek greater wisdom;

4. an ethical foundation to advance political, economic, and social justice and peace;

5. formative practices to shape attention and agency beyond systems, leading to corrective changes through reformation, resistance, and rejection.

Tegmark's ultimate vision for the future of life is something beyond humanity as we know it. Life 3.0 is a disembodied transhuman form of life. "The conventional wisdom among artificial intelligence researchers," Tegmark claims, "is that intelligence is ultimately all about information and computation, not about flesh, blood or carbon atoms." With AI, then, Tegmark believes life can be fully virtualized—still requiring some sort of physical hardware, such as a robot or servers—and preserved as an information pattern that is largely substrate-independent.[58] Even if such an artificial simulation of life were possible at some point in the future, many might find this a reductive version of human intelligence and life as well as an impoverished product of the apocalyptic imagination. In *God, Human, Animal, Machine: Technology, Metaphor, and the Search for Meaning*, Meghan O'Gieblyn observes

> Despite all it has borrowed from Christianity, transhumanism is ultimately fatalistic about the future of humanity. Its rather depressing gospel message insists that we are inevitably going to be

57. Tegmark, *Life 3.0*, 330–31.
58. Tegmark, *Life 3.0*, 55.

superseded by machines and that the only way we can survive the Singularity is to become machines ourselves.[59]

Futures that imagine the end of humanity can be answered with better apocalyptic messages and visions of the future. Rather than superseding it, AI provides opportunities for augmenting human intelligence.

In "How AI Fails Us," a group of scholars critique the dominant view of AI that sees human intelligence as something to be replaced rather than augmented. The replacement strategy, focused on moving toward AGI and ASI, requires the centralization of significant financial and computational resources (e.g., at corporations such as Alphabet/Google and Meta/Facebook) and elevates "optimization protocols over human judgement." While this approach to AI has produced some successful systems, due to a lack of human oversight and accountability it also bears "significant responsibility for today's polarized, low-trust, and highly misinformed political environment." This approach also distracts from and competes with alternative approaches to information automation that have created personal computers, the internet, search engines, and social networking. The authors of the report argue that a more pluralistic approach to AI is needed—one that creates a more diverse ecosystem that complements human intelligence instead of a singular(ity) eschatology. Intelligence is a collective activity, so "[s]ystems that aim to achieve something like the intelligence perceived in humans will thus depend on their capacity for interdependence, sociality, and collective memory, not autonomy." To realize the full potential of AI requires "a proliferation of technological imagination and broad community involvement."[60] Tegmark is right that we need places for conversations about imagined and desired futures—institutions such as the Organization for New Eschatology (ONE), which is created in Neal Stephenson's 2019 novel *The Fall: Or, Dodge in Hell*, to reimagine human futures in a world that realizes the transhuman dream of digitally extending consciousness into a new "Bitworld."[61]

59. O'Gieblyn, *God, Human, Animal, Machine*, 73.
60. Siddarth et al., "How AI Fails Us," 1–2, 8.
61. See Stephenson, *Fall*.

Apocalypse Now

In our memories of the past, anticipations of the future, and perceptions of the present, we are entangled with technology: We shape it as it shapes us. When this goes well, technological change augments us; when it does not, technological change is more like an amputation. Our current interactions with automated and autonomous systems—whether conceived of as a fourth industrial revolution, a fourth modern scientific revolution, or a fourth information revolution—constitute a unique period of profound and transformative change for us and our world. We have been digitally naïve about the dynamics of this period of change for too long, and we need to upgrade our understanding and use of transformative information technologies such as AI so we can augment our lives and actions wisely with intelligence automation. As we begin to imagine new futures—critiquing the "not this" of our present reality as well as seeking the "not yet" of desired futures—the apocalyptic imagination is a generative resource capable of transforming how we think about and use AI. The apocalyptic imagination can enable us to discover ways artificial agency may participate in new creation and to see our present technological transformation as a transformation driven by more than our own new creations.

Epilogue
Reimagining the Present

The Call

In *The Robot Will See You Now*, John Wyatt acknowledges that we face a "unique opportunity for creative thought and engagement as a Christian community" in "the strange new world in which we find ourselves."[1] Floridi observes that "the technophile and the technophobe"—the lover and the fearer of technology—"ask the same question: what's next?" But a deeper question, he says, is "what lies behind"? "Is there a unifying perspective" from which new technological phenomena may be interpreted? Floridi says the problem is that we are still looking at digital information and communication technologies such as AI "as tools for interacting with the world and with each other," when in fact we are transforming the world into an increasingly AI-friendly environment in which interfaces with technology are becoming integral and transparent to us. Many modern philosophical critiques of technology focus on the mechanical and mechanistic culture of the first two industrial revolutions. Today, we also must critically engage a new informational culture and reality shaped by automated information processing. Floridi calls for "an environmental approach" to address new ethical challenges and for formulating ethical frameworks. This requires a "critical review of our current narratives" as well as creating new narratives. Acknowledging the hard work and many challenges ahead, Floridi sees "a great opportunity for our future."[2] Thinking beyond what Le Guin calls "Techno-Heroic" killer stories, we need stories of "creation

1. Wyatt, "Being Human in a World of Intelligent Machines," in Wyatt and Williams, *Robot Will See You Now*, 72.

2. Floridi, *Fourth Revolution*, vi–vii, 218–19.

and transformation"—narratives that redefine technology as part of "the life story."[3] One of the 2021 recommendations from the G20 Interfaith Working Group is for religious groups to create narratives about how AI fits "into their religious worldviews."[4]

These narratives must include the significant social challenges we face. In *The Upswing*, Putnam and Garrett point out startling similarities between US society in the late nineteenth century and today. In the so-called Gilded Age, "Inequality, political polarization, social dislocation, and cultural narcissism prevailed—all accompanied, as they are now, by unprecedented technological advances, prosperity, and material well-being." To address the challenges and opportunities created by the first two industrial revolutions, there was "a holistic reorganizing of society . . . based on a reinvigoration of shared values." This "soul-searching" and social revolution "began at the bottom," was led by youth who "believed that the logic of a bygone era could never speak to the challenges of a completely altered world," and "was both inspired and fueled by ministers and theologians who not only encouraged individuals to change but called upon religious institutions to more actively critique the 'social sins' of the age." Reacting against "individualism, laissez-faire, and inequality," the progressive movement of the early twentieth century "managed to fashion slow and steady reforms as an alternative to calls for revolution" in more violent forms. As was done then, Putnam and Garrett urge, "We must undertake a reevaluation of our shared values—asking ourselves what personal privileges and rights we might be willing to lay aside in service of the common good, and what role we will play in the shared project of shaping our nation's future."[5] Our current social-technological challenges are not of course limited to specific nations. We have created digital information and communication technologies with global integrations, scale, and impacts that require global projects and plans.

The information narratives we need to create now are about becoming postdigital. That digital information and communication technologies are not merely extensions of us but rather deeply integrated with our reality is more of a descriptive statement than a prescriptive or predictive one. Soon, the descriptor "digital" will lose its salience. We will be on the other side of digital transformation, realizing even more of the dynamics of the

3. Le Guin, *Always Coming Home*, 728.
4. G20 Interfaith Working Group, *An Inclusive Global Conversation*.
5. Putnam and Garret, *Upswing*, 8, 130, 329–30, 334, 336.

information automation revolution. Becoming postdigital is not concerned merely with engaging the future being shaped by automated and intelligent technologies now: it concerns being critical about how we are shaping technologies such as AI in the present and how we desire to be shaped by them—or not—while attending to the virtues of hope, faith, and love.[6]

Information automation is an extension of our ancient imaginative drives and desires. This book has argued that AI has already shaped our apocalyptic imagination, often in negative ways, and that the apocalyptic imagination may further—and hopefully in more constructive and positive ways—shape the increasing automation of intelligence. As we become postdigital, temporally and critically, we can expect intelligence automation to augment our apocalyptic imagination about the future, our wisdom, and our vocation in the world.

A Response

At the center of the Lord's Prayer, attention is turned from the transcendent reality of God in heaven to God's immanent presence on earth: the prayer is for God's kingdom to come and God's will to be done "on earth as it is heaven" (Matt 6:10). Weil said that here "we turn our attention back to ourselves in order to compel ourselves to make these petitions a real and not imaginary act."[7] To pray for God's kingdom to come to earth is to pray a prayer that has been and is being answered. Wright says:

> The putting right of all creation has begun. Jesus's people, themselves having been put right, are to live as signposts to God's final new creation. . . . despite the chorus of skepticism, the world really has changed. It is still changing. God's kingdom is coming on earth as in heaven—in the ways Jesus said it would, through the pure in heart, the meek, the mourners, the people hungry for justice, and so on. And these changes are signposts to the ultimate transformation, when Jesus comes again to implement fully and finally the victory he won on the cross, the victory whose most stunning immediate result was his own resurrection.[8]

6. See Knox, "What Does the 'Postdigital' Mean for Education?"
7. Weil, *Waiting for God*, 151.
8. Wright, *On Earth As It Is in Heaven*, xii.

Charles Williams, reflecting on the relationship between the "*Now* and the consequent *Then*"—"not what ought to be, but what *are*"—declared, "'The conversion of time by the Holy Ghost' is the grand activity of the Church." "The Kingdom—or, apocalyptically, the City—is the state" into which the church is called.[9] What this looked like for the early church is recorded in part in the book of Acts, in which "the curtain is drawn back" on the early church's emergence in a new world. Acts "speaks of a revolution," Willie James Jennings declares, of the "insurgency of the Spirit." The book "announces a beginning" and "renders . . . a God who is working, moving, creating the dawn that will break each day, putting into place a holy repetition that speaks of the willingness of God to invade our every day and our every moment." The narrative of Acts is a witness of "how one discerns God's movement" in a world transformed by the love revealed in and through Christ's apocalyptic life and how Christians participate in that movement.[10]

Acts is not merely an "artifact" of "knowledge acquisition and accumulation" for "archival speculations," Jennings observes. Acts "beckons us to a life-giving historical consciousness that senses being in the midst of time that is both past and present and that pulls us toward a future with God in the new creation." And it "reveals the Spirit, who joins us in time, sharing our spaces and partaking in the places we inhabit as places fit for divine activity." Read and experienced this way, Acts shows the early church resisting the oppressive imperial Roman vision of the city as well as cultic withdrawal from the city. The "spatial history" of Acts communicates a historical alternative to Roman rule (empire) and religious retreat (diaspora): "the futures of Israel and the Gentiles are being drawn toward a new destiny in God."[11] The new community and commons into which Jesus calls his followers collapses the destinies of empire and diaspora—the models that prompted his confused disciples to ask the risen Christ, "is this the time when you will restore the kingdom to Israel?" (Acts 1:6)—to reveal and realize a new type of city.

Acts begins in the city of Jerusalem and with the ascension of Jesus. With the intersecting descent of the Spirit, the works of God are proclaimed in many languages at Pentecost. The good message about Jesus is heard by and interpreted for people from "every nation under heaven," and

9. Williams, *Descent of the Dove*, 15.

10. Jennings, *Acts*, 17–18.

11. Jennings, *Acts*, 19–25.

it concerns a new world that is disrupting current social orders and systems (2:5). The present culture is corrupt—it is a "crooked generation" (2:40)—and the "trajectory of the text," and of the lives of those in it, becomes one of "formation." Jerusalem will be destroyed in the near future by the Romans, but the foundations for New Jerusalem laid there and in other cities in and beyond the text will endure through "the apostles' teaching and communion, the sharing in meals, and prayer."[12]

As the narrative of Acts expands geographically, a range of historical memories and future expectations are connected with this movement to "give all people sight of a new creation," a good end and a new beginning. An Ethiopian eunuch finds a destiny that transcends his identity (8:26–39). Saul, who caused many to suffer to protect what he thought was right, will (as Paul) suffer so that others may know what is right (9:1–30). An enslaved fortune-teller is freed to find her own voice (16:16–19). Athenian knowledge and techniques are used to point toward new knowledge and agency (17:16–34). Many Ephesians and others turn away from idolatrous production and consumptions (19:21–41). And citizens of various cities find a new form of citizenship. As Jennings puts it, "All peoples may have a new future in Jesus, and each one of us have a new story to tell that changes the end we previously expected." This end also challenges our previous and current experiences with the established order. Jennings reminds us, "Readers of this text must always remember to humanize this opposition, not in order to soften its tensions but to see into its depth so that we might more clearly grasp its historical trajectory that reaches to us at this moment."[13]

At the end of Acts, as he moves through political systems in Jerusalem and Rome, Paul models a new way of being in the world as a "disciple citizen"—negotiating a "tight space between diaspora fear and state power while remaining focused on the work ahead." "The disciple of Jesus is already of the new order," Jennings explains, "already embodied revolution, already geared to perform rebellion in the everyday acts of living, sharing, and supporting others." And "[t]he purpose of citizenship for a disciple of Jesus is to use the emperor's gold to break the emperor's hold on lives . . . pressing the inner logics of every nation toward good ends for the sake of a suffering creation." By the end of Acts, it is clear that

> God's reign has begun, which means the end of empire, not through sedition but through resurrection. The end of empire is

12. Jennings, *Acts*, 42.
13. Jennings, *Acts*, 42, 47, 129.

the end of the desire for empire. No one can end empire. Only an alternative desire ends it.

Thus, Jennings observes, we "must pay attention to places because our presence carries a call to love our neighbors and our neighborhoods" and we must recognize "that the Spirit of God may be calling us to break with a geographic pattern or help create a new one." Jennings concludes his commentary wondering if we have fully entered into the new beginning announced in Acts.[14]

Christ's revolution of love, driven by the "insurgency of the Spirit" and embodied in his followers, continues—and continues to draw the world further into new creation. Inspired by the apocalyptic imagination, the earliest Christians transformed their imperial cities and technological society by attending to God's presence and work in the knowledge and systems of antiquity. With the same resources, augmented by new powers associated with intelligence automation, we may participate in the transformation of our present technological society. Digital transformation is creating increasingly complex and powerful "empires of AI," and there will be new forms of Babylonian technologies with which we must contend.[15] But the Apocalypse reminds us that the imperial world is passing away, and reveals that technology can drive alternative revolutions as we live more fully into the reality of New Jerusalem. Both ancient and digital wisdom have value as we discern—perhaps with the help of apocalyptic scorecards—constructive actions and collaborations for a better postdigital world and future.

14. Jennings, *Acts*, 154, 166–67, 181, 183, 187.
15. Crawford, *Atlas of AI*, 21.

Bibliography

Alexander, Robert, and Christine Isager, eds. *Fear and Loathing Worldwide: Gonzo Journalism Beyond Hunter S. Thompson*. New York: Bloomsbury Academic, 2018.

Allen, Diogenes. *Spiritual Theology: The Theology of Yesterday for Spiritual Help Today*. Cambridge: Cowley, 1997.

Amazon. "Amazon re:MARS." https://www.youtube.com/channel/UCgkkeHebGYy7udnk NAeBvow.

———. "We're at the Beginning of a Golden Age of AI: Jeff Bezos." January 19, 2019. https://blog.aboutamazon.in/our-business/were-at-the-beginning-of-a-golden-age-of-ai-jeff-bezos.

Anderson, Janna, and Lee Rainie. "The Future of Well-Being in a Tech-Saturated World." Pew Research Center, April 17, 2018. http://www.pewinternet.org/2018/04/17/the-future-of-well-being-in-a-tech-saturated-world/.

Ando, Clifford. "The Children of Cain." In *Urban Religion in Late Antiquity*, edited by Asuman Lätzer-Lasar and Emiliano Rubens Urciuoli, 51–67. Boston: Walter de Gruyter, 2021.

Ashton, John. *The Gospel of John and Christian Origins*. Minneapolis: Fortress, 2014.

Augustine. *Concerning the City of God against the Pagans*. Translated by Henry Bettenson. New York: Penguin, 1972.

———. *Confessions*. Translated by R. S. Pine-Coffin. New York: Penguin, 1961.

Aune, David E. *Revelation 17–22*. The Word Biblical Commentary. Nashville: Thomas Nelson, 1998.

Auxier, Brooke, et al. "10 Tech-Related Trends That Shaped the Decade." Pew Research Center, December 20, 2019. https://www.pewresearch.org/fact-tank/2019/12/20/10-tech-related-trends-that-shaped-the-decade/.

Bacon, Francis. *The Advancement of Learning*. Auckland: Floating, 2010.

———. *New Atlantis*. In *Three Early Modern Utopias: Utopia, New Atlantis, and The Isle of Pines*, edited by Susan Bruce, 149–86. Oxford: Oxford University Press, 2008.

Bauckham, Richard. *The Theology of the Book of Revelation*. Cambridge: Cambridge University Press, 1993.

Becker, Paula, and Alan J. Stein. *The Future Remembered: The 1962 Seattle World's Fair and Its Legacy*. Seattle: Seattle Center Foundation, 2011.

Benjamin, Ruha. *Race After Technology: Abolitionist Tools for the New Jim Code*. Medford, MA: Polity, 2019.

Bennett, Jana Marguerite. *Aquinas on the Web? Doing Theology in an Internet Age*. New York: T & T Clark, 2012.

———. "In the Beginning, Who Created? A Discussion of Theology, Identity, and Social Media." Seattle Pacific University, November 3, 2015. http://digitalcommons.spu.edu/digital_wisdom_framework/.

Berger, Knute. "Introduction." In *Seattle: Past to Present* by Roger Sale, ix–xx. Seattle: University of Washington Press, 2019.

Bezos, Jeff. *Invent and Wonder: The Collected Writings of Jeff Bezos.* Boston: Harvard Business Review and Basic, 2021.

Biro, Dora, et al. "Tool Use as Adaptation." *Philosophical Transactions of the Royal Society B* 368:1630 (2013). https://doi.org/10.1098/rstb.2012.0408.

Blömer, Michael. "Sacred Spaces and New Cities in the Byzantine East." In *Urban Religion in Late Antiquity,* edited by Asuman Lätzer-Lasar and Emiliano Rubens Urciuoli, 205–24. Boston: Walter de Gruyter, 2021.

Blount, Brian K. *Can I Get a Witness?: Reading Revelation through African American Culture.* Louisville: Westminster John Knox, 2005.

———. *Revelation: A Commentary.* Louisville: Westminster John Knox, 2009.

Blum, Edward J. *W. E. B. Du Bois: American Prophet.* Philadelphia: University of Pennsylvania Press, 2009.

Bonhoeffer, Dietrich. *Ethics.* Translated by Reinhard Kraus, et al. Minneapolis: Fortress, 2015.

Borges, Jorge Luis. "Kafka and His Precursors." In *Selected Non-Fictions,* 363–65. New York: Viking, 1999.

———. *Selected Non-Fictions.* New York: Viking, 1999.

Borgmann, Albert. "Introduction." In *Power Failure: Christianity in the Culture of Technology,* 7–8. Grand Rapids: Brazos, 2003.

———. *Power Failure: Christianity in the Culture of Technology.* Grand Rapids: Brazos, 2003.

Boring, M. Eugene. *Hearing John's Voice: Insights for Teaching and Preaching.* Grand Rapids: Eerdmans, 2019.

Bort, Julie. "Jeff Bezos Explains Why the Library in His House Has Two Fireplaces with Two Inscriptions: 'Dreamers' and 'Builders.'" *Business Insider,* June 6, 2019. https://www.businessinsider.com/jeff-bezos-explains-why-his-library-2-fireplaces-2-mottos-2019-6.

Brinkley, Douglas. "Editor's Note." In *The Proud Highway: Saga of a Desperate Southern Gentleman, 1955–1967,* xxi–xxx. London: Bloomsbury, 1997.

Brockman, John, ed. *Possible Minds: 25 Ways of Looking at AI.* New York: Penguin, 2019.

Brueggemann, Walter. *Genesis: Interpretation, A Bible Commentary for Teaching and Preaching.* Louisville: Westminster John Knox, 2005.

Bryson, Joanna J. "The Past Decade and Future of AI's Impact on Society." In *Towards a New Enlightenment? A Transcendent Decade,* 127–59. Open Mind, 2019.

Burdett, Michael S. *Eschatology and the Technological Future.* London: Routledge, 2015.

Burgess, John T. F., and Emily J. M. Knox, eds. *Foundations of Information Ethics.* Chicago: American Library Association, 2019.

Butler, Philip. "Beyond the Live and Zoomiverse: Recognizing Opportunities for Spiritual Connection Outside Live Preaching/Church." In *Ecclesiology for a Digital Church* edited by Heidi A. Campbell and John Dyer, 155–66. London: SCM, 2021.

———. *Black Transhuman Liberation Theology: Technology and Spirituality.* New York: Bloomsbury Academic, 2020.

————. "Introduction." In *Critical Black Futures: Speculative Theories and Explorations*, edited by Philip Butler, 1–18. Singapore: Palgrave Macmillan, 2021.

Čapek, Karel. *R.U.R. (Rossum's Universal Robots)*. Translated by Claudia Novack. New York: Penguin, 2004.

Cave, Stephen, et al., eds. *AI Narratives: A History of Imaginative Thinking about Intelligent Machines*. Oxford: Oxford University Press, 2020.

Cole-Turner, Ron. *The End of Adam and Eve: Theology and the Science of Human Origins*. Pittsburgh: TheologyPlus, 2016.

Collins, John J. *The Apocalyptic Imagination: An Introduction to Jewish Apocalyptic Literature*. Grand Rapids: Eerdmans, 2016.

————, ed. *The Encyclopedia of Apocalypticism: Volume 1, The Origins of Apocalypticism in Judaism and Christianity*. New York: Continuum, 2000.

————. "From Prophecy to Apocalypticism: The Expectation of the End." In *The Encyclopedia of Apocalypticism: Volume 1, The Origins of Apocalypticism in Judaism and Christianity*, 129–51. New York: Continuum, 2000.

————. "General Introduction." In *The Encyclopedia of Apocalypticism: Volume 1, The Origins of Apocalypticism in Judaism and Christianity*, vii–xii. New York: Continuum, 2000.

————, ed. *The Oxford Handbook of Apocalyptic Literature*. Oxford: Oxford University Press, 2014.

————. "What Is Apocalyptic Literature?" In *The Oxford Handbook of Apocalyptic Literature*, edited by John J. Collins, 1–16. Oxford: Oxford University Press, 2014.

Collins, Samuel Gerald. *All Tomorrow's Cultures: Anthropological Engagements with the Future*. New York: Berghahn, 2021.

Cook, Stephen L. "Apocalyptic Prophecy." In *The Oxford Handbook of Apocalyptic Literature*, edited by John J. Collins, 19–35. Oxford: Oxford University Press, 2014.

Coolidge, Frederick L., and Thomas Wynn. *The Rise of Homo Sapiens: The Evolution of Modern Thinking*. Oxford: Oxford University Press, 2018.

Coolman, Boyd Taylor. *The Theology of Hugh of St. Victor: An Interpretation*. Cambridge: Cambridge University Press.

Cornelius, Misha. "Bryan Stevenson to Howard Graduates: 'Hope Is Our Superpower.'" *The Dig*, May 8, 2021. https://thedig.howard.edu/all-stories/bryan-stevenson-howard-graduates-hope-our-superpower.

Cosden, Darrell. *A Theology of Work: Work and the New Creation*. Eugene, OR: Wipf & Stock, 2004.

Crawford, Kate. *Atlas of AI: Power, Politics, and the Planetary Costs of Artificial Intelligence*. New Haven: Yale University Press, 2021.

Crawford, Kate, and Vladan Joler. "Anatomy of an AI System: The Amazon Echo As An Anatomical Map of Human Labor, Data, and Planetary Resources." AI Now Institute and Share Lab, September 7, 2018. https://anatomyof.ai.

Cummings, BJ. *The River That Made Seattle: A Human and Natural History of the Duwamish*. Seattle: University of Washington Press, 2020.

Dafoe, Allan, Yoram Bachrach, Gillian Hadfield, Eric Horvitz, Kate Larson, and Thore Graepel. "Cooperative AI: Machines Must Learn to Find Common Ground." *Nature* 593 (2021) 33–36.

Damasio, Antonio. *The Strange Order of Things: Life, Feeling, and the Making of Culture*. New York: Pantheon, 2018.

Danaher, John. *Automation and Utopia: Human Flourishing in a World without Work.* Cambridge: Harvard University Press, 2019.

Darch, Peter. "Data Ethics." In *Foundations of Information Ethics,* edited by John T. F. Burgess and Emily J. M. Knox, 77–90. Chicago: American Library Association, 2019.

deSilva, David A. *Discovering Revelation: Content, Interpretation, Reception.* Grand Rapids: Eerdmans, 2021.

Diamond, Krista, et al. "How Las Vegas Locals Really Feel about 'Fear and Loathing.'" *Electric Literature,* April 20, 2021. https://electricliterature.com/how-las-vegas-natives-really-feel-about-fear-and-loathing-hunter-s-thompson/.

Dillon, Grace L., ed. *Walking the Clouds: An Anthology of Indigenous Science Fiction.* Tucson: The University of Arizona Press, 2012.

Ditommaso, Lorenzo. "Apocalypticism and the Popular Culture." In *The Oxford Handbook of Apocalyptic Literature,* edited by John J. Collins, 473–510. Oxford: Oxford University Press, 2014.

Dostoevsky, Fyodor. *Notes from Underground.* Translated by Mirra Ginsburg. New York: Bantam, 1989.

Du Bois, W. E. B. *The Souls of Black Folk.* In *Writings,* edited by Nathan Higgins, 357–547. New York: Penguin Random House, 1986.

Dunbar-Ortiz, Roxanne. *Not "A Nation of Immigrants": Settler Colonialism, White Supremacy, and a History of Erasure and Exclusion.* Boston: Beacon, 2021.

Drury, Clifford M. "George Frederick Whitworth, Father of Presbyterianism in Washington." *Journal of the Presbyterian Historical Society* 26:1 (1948) 1–10.

Earle, Samuel. "The Timeline We're On Is Even Darker Than 'The Matrix' Envisioned." *The New York Times,* December 23, 2021. https://www.nytimes.com/2021/12/22/opinion/the-matrix-resurrections-internet-dystopia.html.

Eliot, T. S. *The Complete Poems and Plays: 1909–1950.* New York: Harcourt Bruce Jovanovich, 1952.

Ellul, Jacques. *Apocalypse: The Book of Revelation.* New York: Seabury, 1977.

———. *The Meaning of the City.* Eugene, OR: Wipf and Stock, 2003.

———. *The Technological Society.* New York: Alfred A. Knopf, 1964.

Facer, Keri, and Neil Selwyn. "Digital Technology and the Futures of Education: Towards 'Non-Stupid' Optimism." UNESCO Futures of Education Report, 2021. https://unesdoc.unesco.org/ark:/48223/pf0000377071.

Floridi, Luciano. *The Fourth Revolution: How the Infosphere is Reshaping Human Reality.* Oxford: Oxford University Press, 2014.

———. "Introduction: The Importance of an Ethics-First Approach to the Development of AI." In *Ethics, Governance, and Policies in Artificial Intelligence,* edited by Luciano Floridi, 1–4. Cham, Switzerland: Springer, 2021.

———. *The Philosophy of Information.* Oxford: Oxford University Press, 2011.

———. "Why Information Matters." *The New Atlantis* 51 (Winter 2017) 7–16.

Floridi, Luciano, and Josh Cowls. "A Unified Framework of Five Principles for AI in Society." In *Ethics, Governance, and Policies in Artificial Intelligence,* edited by Luciano Floridi, 5–15. Cham, Switzerland: Springer, 2021.

Floridi, Luciano, et al. "How to Design AI for Social Good: Seven Essential Factors." In *Ethics, Governance, and Policies in Artificial Intelligence,* edited by Luciano Floridi, 125–51. Cham, Switzerland: Springer, 2021.

Ford, Martin. *Architects of Intelligence: The Truth about AI from the People Building It.* Birmingham, UK: Packt, 2018.

Fragaszy, D. M., et al. "The Fourth Dimension of Tool Use: Temporally Enduring Artefacts Aid Primates Learning to Use Tools." *Philosophical Transactions of the Royal Society B* 368:1630 (2013). https://doi.org/10.1098/rstb.2012.0410.

Friesen, Steven J. "Apocalypse and Empire." In *The Oxford Handbook of Apocalyptic Literature,* edited by John J. Collins, 163–79. New York: Oxford University Press, 2014.

Frischmann, Brett, and Evan Selinger. *Re-Engineering Humanity.* New York: Cambridge University Press, 2018.

Frykholm, Amy Johnson. "Apocalypticism in Contemporary Christianity." In *The Oxford Handbook of Apocalyptic Literature,* edited by John J. Collins, 441–56. Oxford: Oxford University Press, 2014.

G20 Interfaith Working Group for Research and Innovation on Science, Technology, and Infrastructure. *An Inclusive Global Conversation on Artificial Intelligence.* December 2021. https://www.g20interfaith.org/app/uploads/2020/09/Report_Inter faithAIFINAL.pdf.

Gazzaley, Adam, and Larry D. Rosen. *The Distracted Mind: Ancient Brains in a High-Tech World.* Cambridge: The MIT Press, 2016.

Geraci, Robert M. *Apocalyptic AI: Visions of Heaven in Robotics, Artificial Intelligence, and Virtual Reality.* New York: Oxford University Press, 2010.

Gidley, Jennifer M. *The Future: A Very Short Introduction.* Oxford: Oxford University Press, 2017.

Gilbert, James. *Redeeming Culture: American Religion in an Age of Science.* Chicago: University of Chicago Press, 1997.

Gorman, Michael J. *Reading Revelation Responsibly: Uncivil Worship and Witness: Following the Lamb into the New Creation.* Eugene, OR: Cascade, 2011.

Grafton, Anthony, and Megan Williams. *Christianity and the Transformation of the Book: Origen, Eusebius, and the Library of Caesarea.* Cambridge: Harvard University Press, 2008.

Harari, Yuval Noah. *Homo Deus: A Brief History of Tomorrow.* New York: HarperCollins, 2017.

———. *Sapiens: A Brief History of Humankind.* New York: HarperCollins, 2015.

Haught, John F. *God after Darwin: A Theology of Evolution.* Boulder, CO: Westview, 2008.

———. *The New Cosmic Story: Inside Our Awakening Universe.* New Haven: Yale University Press, 2017.

Hesiod. *Hesiod I: Theogony, Works and Days, Testimonia.* Edited by Glenn W. Most. Cambridge: Harvard University Press, 2018.

Hicks, Mar. "When Did the Fire Start?" In *Your Computer Is on Fire,* edited by Thomas S. Mullaney et al., 11–26. Cambridge: The MIT Press, 2021.

Hogue, David A. *Remembering the Future, Imagining the Past: Story, Ritual, and the Human Brain.* Pilgrim, 2003.

Howe, David Walker. *What Hath God Wrought: The Transformation of America, 1815–1848.* New York: Oxford University Press, 2007.

Hugh of St. Victor. *Didascalicon.* Translated by Jerome Taylor. New York: Columbia University Press, 1991.

Huxley, Aldous. *Brave New World and Brave New World Revisited.* New York: Harper & Brothers, 1960.

———. "Foreword." In *Brave New World and Brave New World Revisited,* xvi–xxiv. New York: Harper & Brothers, 1960.

Illich, Ivan. *In the Vineyard of the Text: A Commentary on Hugh's Didascalicon*. Chicago: The University of Chicago Press, 1991.

Jennings, Willie James. *Acts: A Theological Commentary on the Bible*. Louisville: Westminster John Knox, 2017.

———. *The Christian Imagination: Theology and the Origins of Race*. New Haven: Yale University Press, 2010.

Kafka, Franz. *Aphorisms*. New York: Schocken, 2015.

Kant, Immanuel. *Critique of Pure Reason*. Translated by Paul Guyer and Allen Wood. Cambridge: Cambridge University Press, 2000.

Kantor, Jodi, et al. "Inside Amazon's Employment Machine." *The New York Times*, June 15, 2021. https://www.nytimes.com/interactive/2021/06/15/us/amazon-workers.html.

Kind, Carly. "The Term 'Ethical AI' Is Finally Starting to Mean Something." VentureBeat, August 23, 2020. https://venturebeat.com/2020/08/23/the-term-ethical-ai-is-finally-starting-to-mean-something/.

King, Martin Luther, Jr. *A Call to Conscience: The Landmark Speeches of Dr. Martin Luther King, Jr.* Edited by Clayborne Carson and Kris Shepard. New York: Grand Central, 2001.

———. "I've Been to the Mountaintop." In *A Call to Conscience: The Landmark Speeches of Dr. Martin Luther King, Jr.*, edited by Clayborne Carson and Kris Shepard, 201–23. New York: Grand Central, 2001.

———. *The Papers of Martin Luther King, Jr., Volume VI: Advocate of the Social Gospel, September 1948–March 1963*. Edited by Clayborne Carson, et al. Berkeley: University of California Press, 2007.

———. "Vision of a World Made New." In *The Papers of Martin Luther King, Jr., Volume VI: Advocate of the Social Gospel, September 1948–March 1963*, edited by Clayborne Carson et al., 182–84. Berkeley: University of California Press, 2007.

Kissinger, Henry A., et al. *The Age of AI: And Our Human Future*. New York: Little, Brown, and Company, 2021.

Knox, Jeremy: "What Does the 'Postdigital' Mean for Education?: Three Critical Perspectives on the Digital with Implications for Educational Research and Practice." *Postdigital Science and Education* 1 (2019) 357–70.

Lang, Fritz, dir. *Metropolis*. Paramount Pictures, 1927.

Lange, Greg. "Billboard Reading 'Will the Last Person Leaving SEATTLE—Turn Out the Lights' Appears Near Sea-Tac International Airport on April 16, 1971." HistoryLink.org, June 8, 1999. https://www.historylink.org/File/1287.

Langford, Michael D. "A Theological Framework for Reflection on Artificial Intelligence." In *AI, Faith, and the Future*, edited by Michael J. Paulus, Jr., and Michael D. Langford, 70–94. Eugene, OR: Pickwick, 2022.

Lankes, David. *Forged in War: How a Century of War Created Today's Information Society*. New York: Rowman & Littlefield, 2021.

Le Guin, Ursula K. *Always Coming Home: Author's Expanded Edition*. Edited by Brian Attebery. New York: Penguin, 2019.

Lee, Kai-Fu. *AI Superpowers: China, Silicon Valley, and the New World Order*. Boston: Mariner, 2018.

Lee, Kai-Fu, and Chen Qiufan. *AI 2041: Ten Visions for Our Future*. New York: Currency, 2021.

Letter of Aristeas. In *Old Testament Pseudepigrapha, Volume 2: Expansions of the "Old Testament" and Legends, Wisdom and Philosophical Literature, Prayers, Psalms, and*

Odes, Fragments of Lost Judeo-Hellenistic Works, edited by James H. Charlesworth. New York: Doubleday, 1985.

Levine, Arthur, and Scott Van Pelt. *The Great Upheaval: Higher Education's Past, Present, and Uncertain Future*. Baltimore: Johns Hopkins University Press, 2021.

Levy, David M. *Mindful Tech: How to Bring Balance to Our Digital Lives*. New Haven: Yale University Press, 2016.

Lieberman, Irving. "Library 21: The Dynamics of Recorded Knowledge and Information." *Stechert-Hafner Book News* XVI:8 (April 1962) 93–95.

Lindsey, Hal. *The Late Great Planet Earth*. Grand Rapids: Zondervan, 1970.

Littman, Michael L., et al. "Gathering Strength, Gathering Storms: The One Hundred Year Study on Artificial Intelligence (AI100) 2021 Study Panel Report." Stanford, CA: Stanford University, 2021. http://ai100.stanford.edu/2021-report.

Liu, Yi-Ling. "Sci-Fi Writer or Prophet? The Hyperreal Life of Chen Qiufan." *Wired*, March 8, 2021. https://www.wired.com/story/science-fiction-writer-china-chen-qiufan/.

Lobel, Orly. *The Equality Machine: Harnessing Digital Technology for a Brighter and More Inclusive Future*. New York: Public Affairs, 2022.

Logan, Robert K., with Marshall McLuhan. *The Future of the Library: From Electronic Media to Digital Media*. New York: Peter Lang, 2016.

Luis, Michael. *Century 21 City: Seattle's Fifty Year Journey from World's Fair to World Stage*. Medina, WA: Fairweather, 2012.

Lynch, Michael Patrick. *The Internet of Us: Knowing More and Understanding Less in the Age of Big Data*. New York: Liveright, 2016.

MacGillis, Alec. *Fulfillment: Winning and Losing in One-Click America*. New York: Farrar, Straus and Giroux, 2021.

Markoff, John. *Machines of Loving Grace: The Quest for Common Ground Between Humans and Robots*. New York: Ecco, 2015.

Marty, Martin E. "Future of No Future: Frameworks of Interpretation." In *The Encyclopedia of Apocalypticism, Volume 3*, edited by Stephen J. Stein, 461–84.

Matthews, Graham. "'A Push-Button Type of Thinking': Automation, Cybernetics, and AI in Midcentury British Literature." In *AI Narratives: A History of Imaginative Thinking about Intelligent Machines*, edited by Stephen Cave et al., 237–59. Oxford: Oxford University Press, 2020.

McEneaney, Kevin T. *Hunter S. Thompson: Fear, Loathing, and the Birth of Gonzo*. New York: Rowman & Littlefield, 2016.

McKeen, William. *Outlaw Journalist: The Life and Times of Hunter S. Thompson*. New York: W. W. Norton & Company, 2008.

———. "The Two Sides of Hunter S. Thompson." *Literary Journalism Studies* 4:1 (2012) 7–18.

McLuhan, Marshal. *Essential McLuhan*. Edited by Eric McLuhan and Frank Zingrone. New York: Basic, 1995.

Metzger, Bruce M. *Breaking the Code: Understanding the Book of Revelation*. Revised by David A. deSilva. Nashville: Abingdon, 2019.

Middleton, J. Richard. "A New Earth Perspective." In *Four Views of Heaven*, edited by Michael Wittmer, 65–94. Grand Rapids: Zondervan Academic, 2022.

Midson, Scott A., ed. *Love, Technology, and Theology*. London: T & T Clark, 2020.

Miller, Walter M., Jr. *A Canticle for Leibowitz*. New York: HarperCollins, 2006.

Mitchell, Melanie. *Artificial Intelligence: A Guide for Thinking Humans*. New York: Farrar, Straus and Giroux, 2019.

Moorhead, James. "Apocalypticism in Mainstream Protestantism, 1800 to the Present." In *The Encyclopedia of Apocalypticism, Volume 3: Apocalypticism in the Modern Period and the Contemporary Age*, edited by Stephen J. Stein, 72–107. New York: Continuum, 2000.

Morgan, Murray. *Century 21: The Story of the Seattle World's Fair, 1962*. Seattle: Acme, 1963.

Morgan, Teresa. "Faith and the City in the 4th Century CE." In *Urban Religion in Late Antiquity*, edited by Asuman Lätzer-Lasar and Emiliano Rubens Urciuoli, 69–95. Boston: Walter de Gruyter, 2021.

Mouw, Richard C. *Calvinism in the Las Vegas Airport: Making Connections in Today's World*. Grand Rapids: Zondervan, 2004.

Mullaney, Thomas S. "Your Computer Is on Fire." In *Your Computer Is on Fire*, edited by Thomas S. Mullaney et al., 3–10. Cambridge: The MIT Press, 2021.

Mullaney, Thomas S., et al., eds. *Your Computer Is on Fire*. Cambridge: The MIT Press, 2021.

National Advisory Commission on Libraries. "Technology and Libraries." In *Reader in Library Services and the Computer*, edited by Louis Kaplan, 5–10. Washington, DC: National Cash Register Company, 1971.

North, Paul. *The Yield: Kafka's Atheological Reformation*. Stanford, CA: Stanford University Press, 2015.

Nuttall, Nick. "Apocalypse and Hell: Hunter S. Thompson's American Dream." *Literary Journalism Studies* 4:1 (2012) 103–16.

OECD. "OECD Framework for the Classification of AI Systems." OECD Digital Economy Papers No. 323. Paris: OECD, 2022. https://doi.org/10.1787/cb6d9eca-en.

O'Gieblyn, Meghan. *God, Human, Animal, Machine: Technology, Metaphor, and the Search for Meaning*. New York: Doubleday, 2021.

O'Mara, Margaret. *Cities of Knowledge: Cold War Science and the Search for the Next Silicon Valley*. Princeton: Princeton University Press, 2004.

Ovenden, Richard. *Burning the Books: A History of the Deliberate Destruction of Knowledge*. Cambridge: Belknap, 2020.

Pasquale, Frank. *New Laws of Robotics: Defending Human Expertise in the Age of AI*. Cambridge: Belknap, 2020.

Paulus, Michael J., Jr. "Automation and Apocalypse." In *AI, Faith, and the Future: An Interdisciplinary Approach*, edited by Michael J. Paulus, Jr., and Michael D. Langford, 170–89. Eugene, OR: Pickwick, 2022.

Paulus, Michael J., Jr., Bruce D. Baker, and Michael D. Langford. "A Framework for Digital Wisdom in Higher Education." *Christian Scholar's Review* XLIX:1 (2019) 43–61.

Pena, Stacy. "Stanford Virtual Conference to Focus on COVID-19 and Artificial Intelligence." Stanford News, March 20, 2020. https://news.stanford.edu/2020/03/20/stanford-virtual-conference-focus-covid-19-artificial-intelligence/.

Peters, Benjamin. "How Do We Live Now?" In *Your Computer Is on Fire*, edited by Thomas S. Mullaney et al., 377–84. Cambridge: The MIT Press, 2021.

Peters, John Durham. *The Marvelous Clouds: Toward a Philosophy of Elemental Media*. Chicago: The University of Chicago Press, 2015.

Peterson, Eugene H. *The Message: The New Testament, Psalms, and Proverbs*. Colorado Springs, CO: NavPress, 1996.

———. *Reversed Thunder: The Revelation of John and the Praying Imagination*. New York: HarperCollins, 1991.

Plummer, Thomas W., and Emma M. Finestone. *Rethinking Human Evolution*. Cambridge: The MIT Press, 2018.

Portier-Young, Anathea E. *Apocalypse against Empire: Theologies of Resistance in Early Judaism*. Grand Rapids: Eerdmans, 2011.

Prior, Matthew T. *Confronting Technology: The Theology of Jacques Ellul*. Eugene, OR: Wipf and Stock, 2020.

Provan, Iain. *Discovering Genesis: Content, Interpretation, Reception*. Grand Rapids: Eerdmans, 2016.

Putnam, Robert D., and Shaylyn Romney Garret. *The Upswing: How America Came Together a Century Ago and How We Can Do It Again*. New York: Simon & Schuster, 2020.

Reich, Rob, et al. *System Error: Where Big Tech Went Wrong and How We Can Reboot*. New York: Harper, 2021.

Resseguie, James L. "Narrative Features of the Book of Revelation." In *The Oxford Handbook of the Book of Revelation*, edited by Craig R. Koester, 37–52. Oxford: Oxford University Press, 2020.

Rheingold, Howard. *Net Smart: How to Thrive Online*. Cambridge: The MIT Press, 2012.

Robinson, Charles E. "Introduction." In *Frankenstein: Or, The Modern Prometheus: Annotated for Scientists, Engineers, and Creators of All Kinds* by Mary Shelley, edited by David H. Guston et al., xxiii–xxxv. Cambridge: The MIT Press, 2017.

Rothman, Hal, and Mike Davis. *The Grit Beneath the Glitter: Tales from the Real Las Vegas*. Berkeley: University of California Press, 2002.

Russo, John Paul. *Future Without a Past: The Humanities in a Technological Society*. Columbia: University of Missouri Press, 2005.

Ryholt, Kim, and Gojko Barjamovic, eds. *Libraries before Alexandria*. Oxford: Oxford University Press, 2019.

Sanchez-Taylor, Joy. *Diverse Futures: Science Fiction and Authors of Color*. Columbus: The Ohio State University Press, 2021.

Scheidel, Walter. *Escape from Rome: The Failure of Empire and the Road to Prosperity*. Princeton: Princeton University Press, 2019.

Schwab, Klaus. *The Fourth Industrial Revolution*. New York: Currency, 2016.

Seattle World's Fair 1962: Official Souvenir Program. Seattle: Century 21 Exposition, 1962.

Sehlinger, Bob. *The Unofficial Guide to Las Vegas*. Birmingham, AL: AdventureKeen, 2019.

Shadbolt, Nigel, and Roger Hampson. *The Digital Ape: How to Live (in Peace) with Smart Machines*. London: Scribe, 2018.

Shears, Jonathon, ed. *The Great Exhibition, 1851: A Sourcebook*. Manchester: Manchester University Press, 2017.

Shelley, Mary. *The Last Man*. Lincoln: University of Nebraska Press, 2006.

Shoro, Mike. "Artificial Intelligence Making More Inroads into Las Vegas Casinos." *Las Vegas Review-Journal*, January 11, 2021. https://www.reviewjournal.com/business/conventions/ces/artificial-intelligence-making-more-inroads-into-las-vegas-casinos-2249860/.

Siddarth, Divya, et al. "How AI Fails Us." Edmond J. Safra Center for Ethics at Harvard University, December 1, 2021. https://ethics.harvard.edu/how-ai-fails-us.

Simon, Herbert. "Designing Organizations for an Information-Rich World." In *Computers, Communications, and the Public Interest*, edited by Martin Greenberger, 37–72. Baltimore: Johns Hopkins, 1971.

Smids, Jilles, Sven Nyholm, and Hannah Berkers. "Robots in the Workplace: A Threat to—or Opportunity for—Meaningful Work?" *Philosophy & Technology* 33 (2020) 503–22.

Smith, Justin E. H. *The Internet Is Not What You Think It Is: A History, a Philosophy, a Warning.* Princeton: Princeton University Press, 2022.

———. "It's All Just Beginning." *The Point*, March 23, 2020. https://thepointmag.com/examined-life/its-all-just-beginning.

Soper, Taylor. "Amazon Adds Two New Leadership Principles Just Days before Jeff Bezos Steps Down as CEO." GeekWire, July, 1, 2021. https://www.geekwire.com/2021/amazon-adds-two-new-leadership-principles-just-days-jeff-bezos-steps-ceo/.

Stark, Rodney. *Cities of God: The Real Story of How Christianity Became an Urban Movement and Conquered Rome.* New York: HarperOne, 2007.

Stephenson, Neal. *The Fall: Or, Dodge in Hell.* New York: William Morrow, 2019.

Stone, Brad. *Amazon Unbound: Jeff Bezos and the Invention of a Global Empire.* New York: Simon & Schuster, 2021.

Stone, Peter, et al. "Artificial Intelligence and Life in 2030: One Hundred Year Study on Artificial Intelligence Report of the 2015-2016 Study Panel." Stanford, CA: Stanford University, 2016. http://ai100.stanford.edu/2016-report.

Streitfeld, David, ed. *Hunter S. Thompson: The Last Interview and Other Conversations.* Brooklyn: Melville House, 2018.

Suarez, Michael F., and H. R. Woudhuysen, eds. *The Book: A Global History.* Oxford: Oxford University Press, 2013.

Suddendorf, Thomas, and Andy Dong. "On the Evolution of Imagination and Design." In *The Oxford Handbook of the Development of Imagination,* edited by Marjorie Taylor, 453–67. Oxford: Oxford University Press, 2013.

Supp-Montgomerie, Jenna. *On Earth As It Is in Heaven: Daily Wisdom for Twenty-First Century Christians.* New York: HarperOne, 2022.

———. *When the Medium Was the Mission: The Atlantic Telegraph and the Religious Origin of Network Culture.* New York: New York University Press, 2021.

Tactical Tech. "Technologies of Hope: 100 Responses to the Pandemic." https://techpandemic.theglassroom.org/.

Tasioulas, John. "Artificial Intelligence, Humanistic Ethics," *Dædalus* 151:2 (Spring 2022) 232–43.

Taylor, Marjorie. "Transcending Time, Place, and/or Circumstance: An Introduction." In *The Oxford Handbook of the Development of Imagination,* edited by Marjorie Taylor, 3–10. Oxford: Oxford University Press, 2013.

Tegmark, Max. *Life 3.0: Being Human in the Age of Artificial Intelligence.* New York: Vintage, 2017.

Thomas, John Christopher. *The Apocalypse: A Literary and Theological Commentary.* Cleveland, TN: CPT, 2012.

Thompson, Anita. *Ancient Gonzo Wisdom: Interviews with Hunter S. Thompson.* Cambridge: Da Capo, 2009.

Thompson, Hunter S. *Fear and Loathing in America: The Brutal Odyssey of an Outlaw Journalist, 1968-1976.* New York: Simon & Schuster, 2000.

———. *Fear and Loathing in Las Vegas: A Savage Journey to the Heart of the American Dream.* New York: Vintage, 1989.

———. *The Proud Highway: Saga of a Desperate Southern Gentleman, 1955-1967.* London: Bloomsbury, 1997.

Thrush, Coll. *Native Seattle: Histories from the Crossing-Over Place.* Seattle: University of Washington Press, 2017.

Too, Yun Lee. *The Idea of the Library in the Ancient World.* Oxford: Oxford University Press, 2010.

Toynbee, Arnold. *Lectures on the Industrial Revolution in England: Popular Addresses, Notes, and Other Fragments.* London: Rivingtons, 1884.

Urciuoli, Emiliano Rubens. "A Tale of No Cities." In *Urban Religion in Late Antiquity,* edited by Asuman Lätzer-Lasar and Emiliano Rubens Urciuoli, 15–49. Boston: Walter de Gruyter, 2021.

Valentine, Patrick M. *A Social History of Books and Libraries from Cuneiform to Bytes.* Lanham, MD: Scarecrow, 2012.

Vallor, Shannon. *Technology and the Virtues: A Philosophical Guide to a Future Worth Wanting.* New York: Oxford University Press, 2016.

Venturi, Robert, et al. *Learning from Las Vegas: Facsimile Edition.* Cambridge: The MIT Press, 2017.

Vincent, James. "iRobot's Newest Roomba Uses AI to Avoid Dog Poop." *The Verge,* September 9, 2021. https://www.theverge.com/2021/9/9/22660467/irobot-roomba-ai-dog-poop-avoidance-j7-specs-price.

Volf, Miroslav. *Work in the Spirit: Toward a Theology of Work.* Oxford: Oxford University Press, 1991.

Vonnegut, Kurt. *Player Piano.* New York: Avon, 1971.

Wachowski, Lana, and Lilly Wachowski, dirs. *The Matrix.* Warner Bros, 1999.

Weil, Simone. *Simone Weil.* Edited by Eric O. Springstead. Maryknoll, NY: Orbis, 1998.

———. *Waiting for God.* New York: HarperCollins, 2000.

Welsh, Robert L. *The Presbytery of Seattle, 1858–2005: The "Dream" of a Presbyterian Colony in the West.* N.p.: 2006.

Wendt, Heidi. "Intellectualizing Religion in the Cities of the Roman Empire." In *Urban Religion in Late Antiquity,* edited by Asuman Lätzer-Lasar and Emiliano Rubens Urciuoli, 97–121. Boston: Walter de Gruyter, 2021.

Whitford, Emma. "UNLV President Turns Himself Into an AI." *Inside Higher Ed,* March 2, 2022. https://www.insidehighered.com/news/2022/03/02/unlv-introduces-digital-president-assist-students.

Whitworth, George F. "Retrospect of Half a Century." *The Washington Historical Quarterly* 1:4 (1907) 197–208.

Wildcat, Daniel. "Enhancing Life in a World of Relatives." In *Buffalo Shout, Salmon Cry: Conversations on Creation, Land Justice, and Life Together,* edited by Steve Heinrichs, 269–309. Harrisonburg, VA: Herald, 2013.

Williams, Charles. *The Descent of the Dove: A Short History of the Holy Spirit in the Church.* Vancouver, BC: Regent College, 2002.

Williams, David B. *Homewaters: A Human and Natural History of Puget Sound.* Seattle: University of Washington Press, 2021.

Williams, James. *Stand Out of Our Light: Freedom and Resistance in the Attention Economy.* Cambridge: Cambridge University Press, 2018.

Williams, Robert W. "M. L. King's Abiding Tribute to W. E. B. Du Bois." *Phylon* 56:1 (2019) 134–55.

Woodley, Randy. "Early Dialogue in the Community of Creation." In *Buffalo Shout, Salmon Cry: Conversations on Creation, Land Justice, and Life Together,* edited by Steve Heinrichs, 92–103. Harrisonburg, VA: Herald, 2013.

Woolf, Greg. *The Life and Death of Ancient Cities: A Natural History*. Oxford: Oxford University Press, 2020.

Wright, David E., and Robert E. Snow. "Las Vegas: Metaphysics in the Technological Society." *The Centennial Review* 23:1 (1979) 40–61.

Wright, N. T. *History and Eschatology: Jesus and the Promise of Natural Theology*. London: SPCK, 2019.

————. *On Earth As It Is in Heaven: Through the Year with Tom Wright*. Edited by Oliver Wright. London: SPCK, 2022.

Wu, Tim. *The Attention Merchants: The Epic Scramble to Get Inside Our Heads*. New York: Alfred A. Knopf, 2016.

Wyatt, John. "Being Human in a World of Intelligent Machines." In *The Robot Will See You Now: Artificial Intelligence and the Christian Faith*, edited by John Wyatt and Stephen N. Williams, 57–72. London: SPCK, 2021.

Wyatt, John, and Stephen N. Williams. "Conclusion." In *The Robot Will See You Now: Artificial Intelligence and the Christian Faith*, edited by John Wyatt and Stephen N. Williams, 228–33. London: SPCK, 2021.

————, eds. *The Robot Will See You Now: Artificial Intelligence and the Christian Faith*. London: SPCK, 2021.

Yang, K. Wayne. *A Third University Is Possible*. Minneapolis: University of Minnesota Press, 2017.

Yarbro Collins, Adela. "Apocalypticism and Christian Origins." In *The Oxford Handbook of Apocalyptic Literature*, edited by John J. Collins, 326–39. Oxford: Oxford University Press, 2014.

Printed in the USA
CPSIA information can be obtained
at www.ICGtesting.com
JSHW021715110224
57068JS00003B/197